The Sea-to-Sky Gold Rush Route

A Guide to the Scenic Railway of the White Pass

by Eric L. Johnson

June 1998

Rusty Spike Publishing

Vancouver, British Columbia, Canada

Copyright © Eric L. Johnson, June, 1998
Maps drawn by Lorne H. Nicklason
Layout and Editing by Lorne H. Nicklason
Printed by Hemlock Printers Ltd., Burnaby, B.C.

Canadian Cataloguing in Publication Data:
Johnson, Eric L., (Eric Lennart), 1933-
  The sea-to-sky gold rush route

ISBN number 0-9681976-1-2
 1. White Pass & Yukon Route (Firm)—History. 2. Railroads, Narrow-gage—Yukon Territory—History.
3. Railroads, Narrow-gage—Yukon Territory—Guidebooks. 4. Klondike River Valley (Yukon)—Gold
discoveries. 5. Yukon Territory—Guidebooks.
I. Title.
HE2810.W48J64 1998   385'.52'097191   C98-910389-7

Front Cover: A pair of 90-class locomotives head-end a southbound
excursion train across the trestle at Tunnel Mountain.

Back Cover: A Bennett excursion train pulls into Fraser, B.C., alongside
alpine Fraser Lake. At the far end of the siding can be seen a water tank,
all-important in the steam days, and still used when steam locomotive
No. 73 makes its way to Lake Bennett.

The Sea-to-Sky Gold Rush Route
A Guide to the Scenic Railway
of the White Pass

TABLE OF CONTENTS

MAPS

Introduction

The **White Pass** (properly known as the railway of the White Pass & Yukon Route, but commonly referred to as the "White Pass railway", or its acronym WP&YR) is one of the most colourful pieces of trackage in North America, from both a historic and a scenic viewpoint. Built as part of a transportation system which would serve the developing Klondike goldfield and open up the Yukon Territory, it is one of the best known and most tangible remnants of the last great gold rush, the Klondike rush of 1898.

Known by most as The White Pass, the railway has been dubbed a gold rush narrow gauge; the gold rush was the stampede of men into the Klondike where the greatest placer gold deposit of all time had just been discovered, and narrow gauge refers to any railway where the distance between the rails is less than that seen on standard gauge lines.

In North America most narrow gauge railways have rails laid with the rail heads spaced 36 inches apart. Compared to standard gauge railways which have rails spaced at 56½ inches, narrow gauge railways can be built with tighter curves, narrower cuts, and steeper grades, and rolling stock is smaller and lighter—all contributing to lower construction and outfitting costs, and to suitability for crossing the forbidding coastal mountains of south-eastern Alaska and north-western British Columbia. When the White Pass was being planned in 1898, a number of 36-inch gauge lines across the United States had already been converted to standard-gauge and there was then a surplus of used equipment

available at bargain prices. Because of the isolation of the route, no consideration for interchange with standard gauge railways was given, and combined with the company's limited funding, "slim gauge" was a logical choice.

The 110-mile line—Skagway, Alaska, to Whitehorse, Yukon—was completed in 1900, and the railway operated continuously until 1982 when a recession forced the owners to mothball the railway. With the rise of tourism in the late 1980s, the railway was resuscitated—albeit as a summer-only, passenger-only, operation at first utilizing only the southern twenty miles of trackage. By 1998, traffic had increased to the point where excursions extend to Carcross at mile 67, with hopes for extension right to Whitehorse by the year 2000.

In 1994 the railway of the White Pass and Yukon Route was honoured by the Canadian Society for Civil Engineering and the American Society of Civil Engineers, ranking the railway along with only fourteen other international engineering landmarks such as the Panama Canal, the Quebec Bridge, and the Statue of Liberty—a tribute to the men that financed, engineered, and built the railway.

The Sea-to-Sky Gold Rush Route - A Guide to the Scenic Railway of the White Pass describes this wonderful railway. The book has four parts. First is a list of the many features of the route. The passengers on the vintage railway coaches will learn of the sights and operational features that greet the eye as they travel the line.

The second part of the guide is a brief history of the White Pass, from the fateful meeting in the St. James Hotel in 1898, to the thriving tourist operation of today.

The third part shows WP&YR employees on the job, and the fourth part lists some of the equipment of the railway, from antique coaches to locomotives to work train rolling stock.

The Sea-to-Sky Gold Rush Route is interspersed with archival photos and modern photos, showing early and current operations. All photos are by the author unless indicated otherwise. The maps provide the traveller with a clear perception of the railway's meandering route.

Along the right-of-way, mileposts show the distance from Skagway, and are used for reference in the text and maps. Because track between Skagway and White Pass has been relocated several times, actual mileage to the pass has varied, but mileposts have been left unchanged.

Several references are made to a "turn", such as a Bennett turn or a Fraser turn. This is a train that goes from its home terminal to the intended destination, and returns.

Visitors will develop an appreciation for the rugged simplicity of the White Pass, and leave for home with a richer experience. Armchair travellers will also find reward in this guide, and hopefully be sufficiently inspired to visit the railway.

Acknowledgments
My thanks to Mark Baker, Boerries Burkhardt, Alice Cyr, Tina Cyr, Robert G. Hilton, Carl Mulvihill, John Westfall, Ron Willis, and many other White Pass employees and fans for their help. I also thank my editor Lorne Nicklason for his critical proof-reading and attention to detail, and layout of this book.

Sources
The White Pass, Gateway to the Klondike, by Roy Minter
Annual Reports to the Minister of Railways and Canals, etc. - National Archives, Ottawa
WP&YR Corporate Records - Yukon Archives
WP&YR Annual Reports, 1951 to 1975

This is an exciting day in Skaguay, as the first excursion train prepares to pull out with a full load of enthusiastic passengers. A century later, the trains of the White Pass & Yukon Route still pull out of Skagway with full loads of enthusiastic passengers. Although the trains look a little different now, the route is almost the same.
Vancouver Public Library Photograph Number 9779

THE ROUTE OF THE
WHITE PASS & YUKON ROUTE

Mile 0.0   Skagway At the head of Lynn Canal, Skagway is the southern terminus of the railway of the WP&YR, northern terminus of a number of cruise ship lines, and it was the staging point for gold-seekers of 1898 bound for the Klondike via White Pass.

The first permanent settler on soil which is now part of Skagway was Captain William Moore, a legendary steamboat skipper, who had arrived in the mid-1880s. He learned of the existence of White Pass from the Chilkat Indians and after hacking out a rough trail to the summit he was convinced that it, rather than Chilkoot Pass, would one day be laid with steel rails. Construction of the railway began at Skagway on May 27, 1898, and the last spike was driven at Carcross, Yukon, on July 29, 1900.

Today, there are several historic pieces of WP&YR equipment in Skagway. Steam locomotive No. 52— the first locomotive to reach Skagway, in 1898— can be seen across the street from the WP&YR station. At the Trail of '98 Museum at 7th Avenue and Spring Street in downtown Skagway, steam

locomotive No. 195 is on display. It was one of eleven identical machines brought by the US Army to Skagway in 1943. Parked at the WP&YR depot is an 1899 Cooke rotary snowplow. For years it was in retirement, simply part of a display of obsolete equipment. Then, over the winter of 1995-96, the rotary was rebuilt, and is now used in mid-April to clear snow from the rail grade in the pass area, just prior to start-up of seasonal operations. The rotary is on display in the tourist season.

There are six docks on the Skagway waterfront where cruise ships tie up: on the eastern side of the inlet and at the base of the mountain wall is the Railroad Dock, next is the Boat Harbor which is limited to rather smallish boats, the Ferry Dock where Alaska State Ferries also dock, the Ferry Dock West, the Broadway Dock at the foot of Broadway Street, and the Ore Dock where in earlier times mineral concentrates were loaded on bulk carriers. The largest of cruise ships disembark passengers only at the Railroad, Broadway, and Ore Docks which each have track leading to them.

(Continued on page 4)

1

At the height of the season, as many as four cruise ships may tie up in one day at the Skagway docks. Second and third Summit Excursion trains run on those busy days. Close scheduling of these trains does not permit steam locomotive No. 73 to lead the additional trains to Shops, as seen here where engines 99, 93, and 91 prepare to leave the Broadway Dock.

The **Sun Viking** was one of two dozen cruise ships which made calls at Skagway during 1995. Small, compared to some other ships, it nevertheless carried 726 passengers. Coach No. 258, the **Lake Kluahne**, was built in 1893 and saw first service with the Pacific Coast Railway in California.

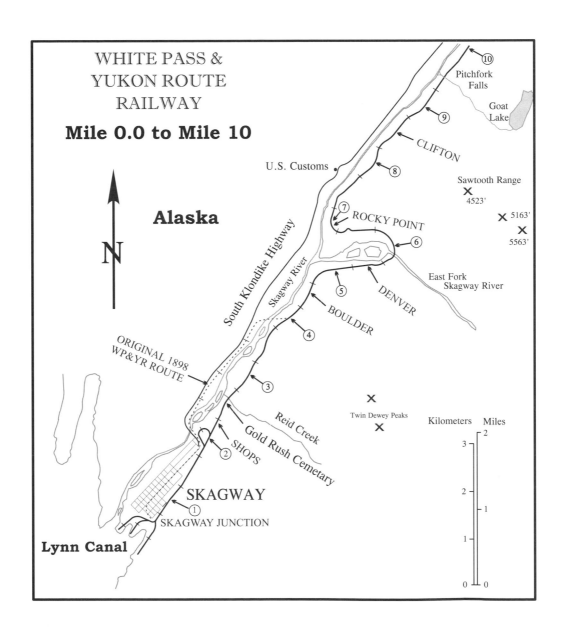

WHITE PASS &
YUKON ROUTE
RAILWAY

Mile 0.0 to Mile 10

Alaska

N

Pitchfork Falls

Goat Lake

⑩

⑨

CLIFTON

⑧

U.S. Customs

Sawtooth Range
✕
4523'

✕ 5163'

✕
5563'

⑦

ROCKY POINT

⑥

DENVER

East Fork
Skagway River

South Klondike Highway

Skagway River

⑤

BOULDER

④

ORIGINAL 1898
WP&YR ROUTE

③

Reid Creek

✕
Twin Dewey Peaks
✕

Gold Rush Cemetary

② SHOPS

SKAGWAY

① SKAGWAY JUNCTION

Lynn Canal

Kilometers   Miles

3

2

1

0

2

1

0

Skagway is a quiet community of about 750 citizens in the off-season, but the resident numbers triple during the summer months, and cruise ships can in one day bring in as many as 8000 more cheerful faces!

In Skagway, the original rail line ran up the centre of Broadway as far as Shops (mile 2), since a proposed tramway company had already pre-empted the strip of land along the foot of the mountain in 1897—the railway was relocated to this, its present line, in 1942.

Mile 1.5 Just south of Shops are coach tracks where active passenger cars are cleaned and stored. In the 1997 season the White Pass had forty-five cars on the roster. Of these, nineteen are relatively new cars built between 1969 and 1993; the remaining twenty-six were built prior to 1937, and No. 244, the **Lake Emerald**, is the oldest, having been built in 1883. All of the older cars have been rebuilt over the years and are in excellent condition.

Mile 2.0 Shops, as the WP&YR's repair and maintenance centre is named, is home to the WP&YR's fourteen active diesel-electric locomotives: General Electric Nos. 90 to 95, 97 to 100, Montreal Locomotive Works Nos. 108, 109, and 110, and Bombardier No. 114. Another engine, No. 96, has been out of service since the 1970s but will be soon back in service. All of the diesel-electrics were built to order for the White Pass.

An excursion train has just returned to Skagway and the engines are being switched to haul the train back to the coach tracks for the night. Brakeman Buddy True controls traffic at the south end of Broadway and gives signals to the engineer.

Then, there is the pride of the fleet—Baldwin Locomotive Works No. 73, a steam locomotive built for the White Pass in 1947! Stored on site also are numerous pieces of maintenance-of-way equipment. Shops no longer has a turntable, so uses a loop track to turn engines if necessary. The original roundhouse and turntable lasted from 1898 until late 1969 when they were destroyed by fire which also claimed two brand-new locomotives and other rolling stock, and damaged a number of other pieces of equipment.

As already mentioned, the original rail line laid in 1898 was forced to take Broadway as far as Shops. There the rail line crossed the Skagway River because another competitor, Brackett's wagon road, had rights to the very narrow strip of land—about two miles in length—between the foot of the mountain and the east bank of the Skagway River. A short stretch of track on the west side of the river brought WP&YR trains to a second trestle at mile 4.0 where the grade crossed back to the east side of the canyon. Tracks were later laid entirely along the east side of the Skagway River, and the trestles were abandoned.

Waiting on the Railroad Dock track with the afternoon Summit Excursion train in tow, No. 73 will leave for Shops in a few minutes. This dock track is the original line to deep water and steamship anchorage that was laid down by Michael Heney's construction crews in 1898.

*Passengers board a train bound for White Pass. With one hand on his watch, mindful of the train schedule, conductor Lee Hartson, Jr., oversees loading. Coaches 206 and 204, the **Lake Nares** and **Lake Chilkoot**, were built in 1993.*

A Lake Bennett Adventure train returns to Skagway. Available from 1992 until 1995, the round trip took five and one-half hours, including a thirty-minute stop at Bennett. To the left are the WP&YR's coach tracks where, after a day's business, all coaches are parked for cleaning in readiness for next day.

Mile 2.5 Gold Rush Cemetery is the resting place of pioneer Skagway residents, and the notorious "Soapy" Smith and his nemesis Frank Reid. The cemetery is a popular attraction for visitors, and headstones are sober reminders of how many young men and women never attained the riches the gold rush had promised.

Mile 2.6 Bridge 2A   A short span, Bridge 2A is a crossing of Reid Creek. Railway bridges are designated by a numeral (which tells within what mile the bridge in located) and a letter ("A" for the first within that mile, "B" for the second, and so on). A few hundred feet up the creek from Bridge 2A is Reid Falls which can be reached by a rough trail.

Mile 3.0   A realignment, in 1991, of the old grade took out several curves and created the longest tangent (a perfectly straight track), 8/10ths of a mile in length, to be found on the American portion of the rail line. Fill along the grade and a shift in the channel of the Skagway River permitted the improvement—trains can make 25 miles per hour here, the fastest speed permitted between Skagway and the White Pass. The abandoned grade can be see at the foot of the mountain, rapidly being overcome by bush.

Mile 4.0   In 1899, the first Boulder station, a 20-car siding, existed here where the original rail line recrossed the Skagway River.

Late in the evening of August 27, 1997, the 800-passenger **Crown Majesty** is moored for the night at the Skagway Ore Dock; it will sail from Skagway in the morning.

Locomotive No. 73, built for the WP&YR in 1947, worked regularly until 1968 when it was retired. In 1982, it was rebuilt to please touring vacationers, and today No. 73 is still the star of the Skagway waterfront. Chuffing back and forth with bell clanging, whistling, and blowing off steam, the old Baldwin thrills tens of thousands every year hauling trains from the docks to Shops.

A northbound afternoon train is just coming off the Skagway depot track, at Skagway Junction. Engines 90 and 91 were the first diesel-electric locomotives acquired by the WP&YR railway in 1954.

Mile 4.5 Boulder Today, Boulder Station is only a sign post used by WP&YR dispatchers for controlling train movements. In the early mornings black bears are frequently seen along this stretch of track, which is hemmed in with trees, since the East Fork of the Skagway River—and its resident fish—is just below the grade. The grade here is still only 210 feet above sea level; the ascent soon begins.

Mile 5.8 Denver at 402 feet above sea level is at the south end of Bridge 5A crossing the East Fork of the Skagway River. A hiking trail splits off to the south-east, destination: the Denver Glacier, 3½ miles up the valley and 2,500 feet higher in elevation. At the foot of the hiking trail on the railway right-of-way, refurbished WP&YR caboose

No. 905 has been parked since spring of 1994 for the benefit of weary hikers; it can be rented for overnight stays through the U.S. Forest Service. Once the train is across the Bridge 5A, the engineer shoves the locomotive throttle to "notch 8" for maximum power—still train speed does not exceed 15 miles per hour, since in the next one mile the grade is a steep 3.5% (a rise of 3.5 feet for every one hundred feet of travel).

Mile 6.9 Rocky Point Trains are now 637 feet above sea level; this was the first heavy rock cut in the rail grade's path enroute to the summit. To the left, just before entering the cut, one can look south and see Skagway and Lynn Canal far below, spread out on the Skagway River delta,

A northbound Bennett turns accelerates across Bridge 2A crossing Reid Creek; the bridge identification system denotes the first bridge between mile 2 and mile 3. Located behind the locomotive is Gold Rush Cemetery.

No. 73 has just finished loading a group of passengers at Skagway Junction, and is accelerating away. At Shops, diesels will take control of the train. Six times a year, the steam locomotive leads excursion trains to Bennett.

lying in a great cleft between mountain buttresses. In 1899 there was a 10-car siding at Rocky Point where the grade once more encountered Brackett's wagon road which had climbed steeply up from the valley, striking the grade at the north end of the rock cut.

Mile 7.1, 7.3, 7.6   Three bridges, 7A, 7B, and 7C, span near-vertical crevices on the canyon wall. Of steel and concrete, the structures and retaining walls are "rock-bolted" into solid bedrock. Train speed here, more than five hundred feet above the river, is restricted to twelve miles per hour.

Mile 8.5   This is the narrowest part of the canyon: on the far side is the U.S. Customs station on the South Klondike Highway—so near (1000 feet as a raven flies) and yet so far away (fourteen miles by rail and pavement).

Mile 8.6   Clifton   At 849 feet above sea level, Clifton was named for the great ledge of rock overhanging several hundred feet of track. Clifton was once the site of a section house where a track maintenance gang was based in the early days. The 792-foot siding is still in use today.

(Continued on page 15)

As part of the railway's track upgrading program, several curves were eliminated in a realignment in 1990-91. The former grade can be seen at the lower right. The returning Fraser turn highballs home at the maximum 25 miles per hour permitted speed.

At the south end of the bridge over the East Fork of the Skagway River is Denver Station. From this spot a trail leads up the valley to the right heading for Denver Glacier, a popular destination for summer hikers. In the spring of 1994 caboose No. 905 was set up as an overnight stop for hikers. Black bears are frequently seen along the stretch of track between mile 3.0 and Denver.

10

A Summit Excursion train, returning home from White Pass, crosses Bridge 5A over the East Fork of the Skagway River. The timetable location known as Denver Station is at the bridge. All 90-class locomotives were delivered to the WP&YR in yellow and green, but most were repainted in the blue and white scheme in 1981 and 1982; those were then repainted in the original yellow and green scheme in the 1990s.

A Skagway-bound Summit Excursion train coasts downgrade at mile 7, as seen from the South Klondike Highway. Hardly 1000 feet away, the highway is separated from the railway by the Skagway River gorge.

Clifton, located beneath a great rock overhang, has always been popular with photographers.

A homeward-bound train crawls across Bridge 7A. The concrete retaining wall and rock bolts are clearly visible at the lower left.

Also seen from the South Klondike Highway are the many cascades of Pitchfork Falls. The train has slowed to five miles per hour to allow passengers to take in the sight.

An uncommon passenger train meet has just occurred at Glacier siding. The second Summit Excursion Train head-ended by No. 94 was very late getting away from the Skagway docks because of the tardy arrival of a tour ship. Normally the two trains would have met at White Pass, but unable to wait there for one hour, the first Summit Excursion headed back south to meet the northbound at Glacier.

Below: Led by the three remaining 101-class locomotives, an afternoon Summit Excursion train is exiting the south portal of the tunnel onto Bridge 15C, which spans Glacier Gorge.

Opposite: The date is February 20, 1899, and the first passenger train over this new section of track poses on the just-completed trestle. Construction was done in the cold, wind, and darkness of the winter of 1898-99.

Yukon Archives, no. 4126

Mile 8.8 Across the canyon, just below the South Klondike Highway, can be seen **ON TO ALASKA WITH BUCHANAN** painted on a cliff face almost eighty years ago by the Buchanan Boys, a touring group sponsored by a philanthropic gentleman of that surname. At that time, there was no road on the far side of the canyon—the "boys" made their way down from the tracks, across the river, and up the far cliffs. The sign has, of course, been touched-up over the years.

Mile 9.4 Leading down from Goat Lake and passing beneath the railway tracks is a penstock carrying water to a hydro-electric plant on the Skagway River far below. Built in 1997 by the Alaska Power and Telephone Company, the plant supplies energy to Skagway.

Mile 9.5 Pitchfork Falls Trains reduce speed for the crossing of Pitchfork Falls, which from the far side of the canyon has the appearance of a many-tined pitchfork. The creek has its origin in Goat Lake, a glacier-fed alpine lake 2000 feet above the rail grade.

Mile 10.2 Black Cross Rock

On August 3, 1898, two construction workers were killed below the grade when a 100-ton rock crashed down on them; the huge slab is clearly visible from the train and is marked as described. The men's bodies were not recovered, and Black Cross marks their resting place, commemorating theirs and the lives of another twenty-eight men lost in construction of the railway.

FIRST PASSENGER TRAIN OVER WHITE PASS AND YUKON ROUTE TO SUMMIT FEB. 20 1899.

15

Nearing Inspiration Point, the afternoon Fraser-bound train works it way up the grade. In the distance are the Sawtooth Mountains, five miles away, with peaks reaching above 7000 feet.

At mile 18.3, engineer John Westfall pilots the Fraser turn past Gulch Station. Prominent in this scene is the original Bridge 18A, completed in 1901 and abandoned in 1969. New Bridge 18A spanning Cut-off Gulch can be seen above the two 90-class diesel locomotives. Immediately on crossing the bridge, north-bound trains plunge into a tunnel, blasted through the mountain buttress at the same time as the new bridge was built.

A morning Summit Excursion train rumbles over the curved spans of Bridge 18A at a restricted speed of 12 miles per hour. The locomotives are working hard upgrade, as can be noted from the smoke streaming from the exhaust stacks. The original Bridge 18A is visible farther down Cut-off Gulch.

Exiting the north portal of the tunnel at mile 18.9, the Fraser turn struggles against the steep gradient.

Mile 11.5   Bridal Veil Falls

These falls can be seen across the canyon of the Skagway River. As many as twenty-two channels, fed by melt-water from glaciers on Mount Cleveland, have been counted in the peak runoff season. The South Klondike Highway passes over the Captain William Moore bridge which spans the major channel, and farther down, the road crosses over another great cascade which generates mist and spray that billows out over the pavement—a welcome spectacle on a hot summer afternoon.

Mile 12.0   While the northbound ruling grade

(the steepest grade on a particular stretch of rail line that governs tonnage limits and engine power requirements) on the railway is listed as 3.9%, in fact a short stretch at mile 12.0 is believed to be

about 4.2%. Speculations blame a mistake in surveying; two grading crews met here on unexpectedly different levels and a short, steeper than calculated, connecting section was the result. Locomotive engineers notice the change—a significant two miles per hour drop in train speed. At this point, trains have entered what has been called the "Glacier Loop", although the Glacier Switchback would be more properly descriptive.

Mile 12.3   Heney   At 1,573 feet above sea

level, Heney Station was named in honour of Michael J. Heney, the general contractor for construction of the rail line. Here, in 1898, a steeply inclined rail line—actually a "tram" line—was built from the grade down to White Pass City on the canyon floor. White Pass City was a short-lived camp, a transfer station where the wagon road

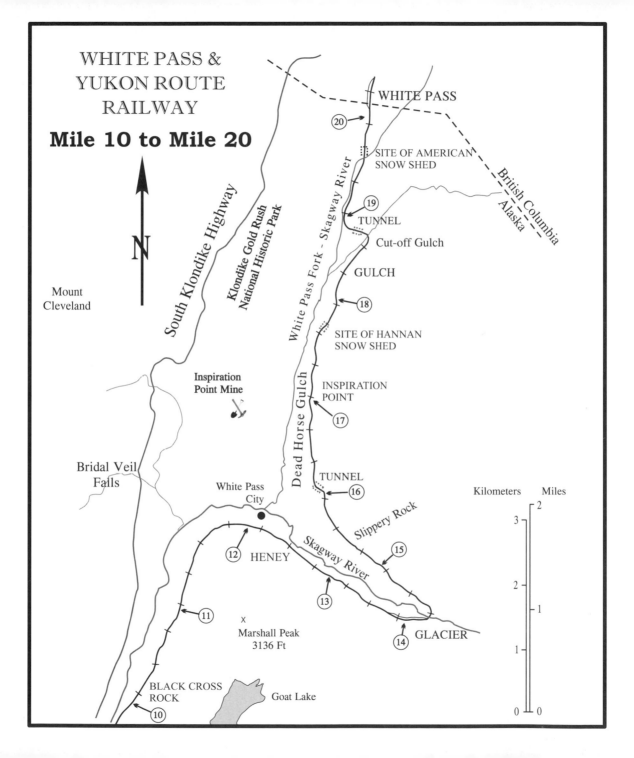

A view of the Sawtooth Range opens up to travellers southbound on leaving the tunnel at mile 15.6. The locomotives are already on a solid concrete fill, rock-bolted to the mountain side—that is Slippery Rock ahead. When first built this section of track was supported by timber trestles.

Opposite: The morning Summit Excursion with a fourteen-coach consist gains speed after leaving the 12-mph speed-restricted Glacier Gorge section.

At mile 16, just south of Inspiration Point, Train No. 24 heads home from White Pass—with dynamic braking, engines 93, 94, and 95 hold back the train on a 3.8% grade. In the photo above, the same train is seen five minutes farther down the line.

Mile 12.4   Bridge 12A This bridge was once a timber trestle, but has been replaced with a steel box girder bridge.

Mile 14.1   Glacier This station, at 1,871 feet above sea level, was once home to a gang of track maintenance men. Today, there is only a box car here which serves as a maintenance-of-way shed, and a 1,332-foot siding—an important piece of trackage where equipment can be stored, and where work trains and passenger trains meet.

At the north end of the siding, Bridge 14A crosses the major fork of the Skagway River which has its origin in Warm Pass only a few miles to the east. Glacier is also the starting point of a very popular hiking trail leading to the Laughton Glacier about 1000 feet higher and two miles by a trail south-easterly. Pesky black bears can often be seen at Glacier, snuffling about for food. However, smells are all they find for train crews and hikers alike abide by a strict rule: no food scraps are left there to encourage the furry scavengers. Brown bears—better known as grizzlies—also visit Glacier. Although far fewer in number than black bears, and of a more reclusive nature, they have not infre-quently been seen, coming down from their favoured haunts far up the mountain side.

Mile 15.6 Slippery Rock
One of the more treacherous rock faces attacked by construction crews, Slippery Rock was an extraordinary obstacle. Workmen tethered by guy lines drilled, blasted, and mucked out a notch in the steeply-sloping granite face to create a bed for the rail grade.

ended and the ignominious Dead Horse Trail of 1897-98 began. However, Brackett had improved the trail by summer of 1898, and freight arriving by wagon here was broken down into smaller lots for packing as far as White Pass. Rail construction men and material were also moved through White Pass City, some to camps over the pass, others to a site at mile 16 on the surveyed rail line which was not yet linked with the grade at mile 12.3. White Pass City was abandoned when rails reached the summit of White Pass.

A Summit Excursion train is approaching Inspiration Point where in earlier years, mixed trains stopped to let passengers step off and enjoy the panorama. In the distant right, Skagway can be seen at the head of Lynn Canal.

On a fine June afternoon, the southbound Summit Excursion train coasts past a small waterfall—one of many to be seen along the right-of-way early in the season. The location is a few hundred feet north of Inspiration Point.

Mile 15.9 Tunnel Mountain

At 2,275 feet above sea level, a spectacular section of the rail line hugs a sheer granite cliff and then crosses a 54-foot high wooden trestle (Bridge 15C) spanning a dry gulch (water does flow in the spring time) just before plunging into a 250-foot tunnel. In the winter of 1898-99, tunnel and bridge crews based at White Pass City plodded and scrambled up to the site, only three quarters of a mile away but 1000 feet higher in elevation. Under extremely adverse conditions—wind, snow, and practically sunless days—tunnel and trestle were completed in February 1899.

Mile 16.9 Inspiration Point

Having cleared the second leg of Glacier Loop, trains break away from the cliffs of Tunnel Mountain, to reach Inspiration Point at 2,475 feet above sea level. In days gone by, Inspiration Point was a welcome fifteen-minute stop where passengers got out to stretch legs and take in the sights—and what sights they are! Looking back to the south-west where the train had been fifteen minutes earlier, Heney Station can be seen less than one flight mile away but almost four track miles distant, and 700 feet lower in elevation. Towering beyond the grade is the serrated Sawtooth Range whose peaks exceed 7000 feet. Down the valley of the Skagway River, Lynn Canal and Skagway come back into view. Across the canyon to the north-west is Mine Mountain. From its bare slopes a cableway, built to serve the Inspiration Point Mine in the late

In July in the early 1990s, the locomotives of the southbound Bennett turn are seen entering the Hannan Snow Shed, named after K.B. Hannan, WP&YR general manager until the early 1950s. The snow shed, in poor condition and no longer necessary during summer-only traffic, was later demolished.

An engineering wonder in its time, the old steel bridge at mile 18.5 was replaced by a far less aesthetic structure, albeit a more substantial-looking one. In use for sixty-eight years the old bridge with its timber approach trestles was deemed inadequate for the heavy freight trains, carrying silver/lead/zinc concentrates, which began running in 1969.

1920s, stretched across the canyon to the railway grade. Only with difficulty can the remains of the silver mine, an unrealized prospect, be spotted.

Mile 17.5 Dead Horse Gulch

At the bottom of the canyon below mile 17.5 lies a section of the White Pass Trail that became known as Dead Horse Gulch. Although advertised as a good trail, this was far from accurate; the trail was a morass, a single-file jumble of bog, water, rocks, and tree roots. Freighters and gold-maddened cheechakos drove hundreds of ill-kept pack animals to their death over the winter and spring of 1897 - 98, earning this wretched section of trail the epithetic label, "Dead Horse Gulch". Brackett did

improve the trail in the summer of 1898, making it practical for packing.

Mile 17.6 Hannan Snow Shed site.

Here on the steep mountain face was the site of the Hannan Snow Shed, demolished in 1992 as it was no longer needed for summer-only railway operation. It was the first of three major snow sheds in the vicinity of the White Pass summit.

Mile 18.3 Gulch
Only a sign post marks Gulch Station, a reference point in controlling traffic. When trains pass the station, the fact is transmitted to other trains to maintain safe distances apart.

Snow still remains in Cut-off Gulch as melt water
tumbles down on its way to the White Pass Fork
of the Skagway River. This view illustrates the
engineering problem faced by Michael Heney when
he laid out the WP&YR grade in 1898. In a few
seconds, Train No.3—the first Summit Excursion—
led by engines 99, 97, and 93 will be high overhead
on the steel bridge at mile 18.6.

Two of the WP&YR's three remaining 1200-
horsepower locomotives lead the daily Summit
Excursion home from White Pass. The old
switchback line ran along the far bank of the gulch,
seen in line with the third coach. Up the gulch,
remains of the switchback are still clearly evident.

In the early 1900s, a double-header (that is, led by two locomotives) passenger train has stopped for the photographer—then, as today, the bridge was a popular sight. At the north end of the bridge can be seen the house which covered the turntable, with sheltered entry doors on both sides. Snow fences are to the left the house, and beyond the train at the upper right.

1342 Yukon Archives/ University of Washington

On the far side of the gulch is the homeward bound Summit Excursion led by engines 91 and 90. Original Bridge 18A is still a marvel.

Mile 18.5 Original Bridge 18A

At 2,755 feet above sea level, the great 215-foot steel cantilever Bridge 18A with wooden approach trestles was abandoned when the White Pass built a new bridge a few hundred feet farther up the gulch. In the days of mixed trains, passengers would crowd the vestibules to gawk and quake at the chasm below as the train rumbled over the bridge at the maximum allowed six miles per hour. Bridge 18A went into service in 1901 and was last used in 1969. As a sort of trade mark, sketches of the bridge have been used on various White Pass logos over the years. Just off the north approach to the bridge was a circular building which sheltered a turntable. The structure can be seen in the photo opposite. The turntable remained in place into the early diesel-electric days, when it was dismantled.

Mile 18.6 New Bridge 18A To handle

heavier trains carrying lead-zinc concentrates led by new heavier-weight locomotives, the less-spectacular but sturdier steel deck plate girder bridge (new Bridge 18A) was built a few hundred feet farther up the gulch in 1969. At the north end of the bridge a 675-foot tunnel was driven through the mountain spur, and a few hundred feet beyond the tunnel's north portal the new rail line was rejoined with the old.

Mile 19.3 Trail of '98 One-quarter mile

beyond the north portal of the tunnel the rail grade is blasted out of a rock cliff, and below (to the northwest) can be seen the valley bottom steeply rising to join the rail grade. Across the now-shallow gulch is a remnant of the old White Pass Trail, marked by a sign-post. Infamous Dead Horse Gulch lay behind. The trail was part of the route promoted by Captain Moore, and the final leg of Brackett's wagon road, one of the two major pre-railway routes to the Klondike across the coastal mountains. The other major route was, of course, Chilkoot Pass only six miles north-westerly.

Mile 19.4 American Snow Shed site

As the rail grade approaches the summit, the adjacent rock walls become less precipitous and small ponds, the source of the small creek in the gulch, come into view—snow lingers here all summer in some years. An inhospitable wind-swept notch in winter, this was the site of the American Snow Shed until the late 1980s when it was demolished.

Mile 20.4   White Pass   This railway station

lies at the summit, 2,856 feet above sea level, on the boundary between Alaska, U.S.A., and British Columbia, Canada. In fact, at the time of rail construction the boundary had not yet been determined; not until the early 1900s was the line officially defined. The pass was named in 1888 by William Ogilvie, Dominion Land Surveyor, "in honour of the late Hon. Thos. White, Minister of the Interior" who was Ogilvie's superior. Ten years before the great gold rush, the Canadian Government had sent Ogilvie into the North to determine feasible access routes into the Yukon District, to make surveys, and to determine the boundary line between Canadian and American territory. At the time the route to the interior over Chilkoot Pass was in moderate use, but White Pass was barely known. Captain William Moore, first settler at what would become Skagway, had informed Ogilvie of the lower—and a supposedly easier—packing route, White Pass.

(Continued on page 31)

27

THREE CROSSINGS OF CUT-OFF GULCH
1899, 1901, 1969

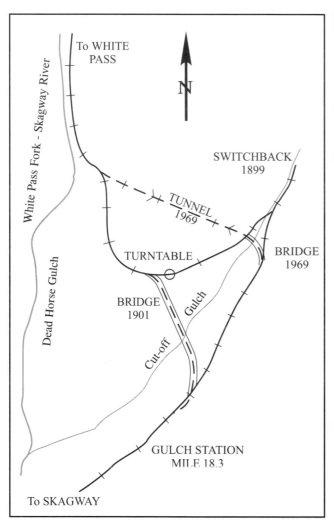

To WHITE PASS

N

White Pass Fork - Skagway River

SWITCHBACK
1899

TUNNEL
1969

Dead Horse Gulch

TURNTABLE

BRIDGE
1969

BRIDGE
1901

Cut-off Gulch

GULCH STATION
MILE 18.3

To SKAGWAY

Cut-off Gulch has been spanned in three places since 1899. The first passenger train to reach White Pass (on February 20, 1899) crossed the gulch well up from the later sites of the two steel bridges. This interim crossing was a simple installation, a switch-back and turntable, necessary only until original Bridge 18A was completed in 1901. While the train movement over the installation was simple, it was time-consuming, taking trains twenty minutes to cover the two miles from Switchback to White Pass.

A northbound train proceeded as follows:
1) the train pulled onto the tail of the switchback
2) the switch was reversed, and the train backed up, crossing Cut-off Gulch on a low trestle
3) the train was shoved across the turntable
4) the locomotive was cut off the train, moved back onto the turntable, and turned 180 degrees so it was once more facing north
5) the locomotive recoupled to the train, and shoved the train up to White Pass (All cars were now strung in the reverse order from what they had been on arriving at Switchback.)
6) at White Pass, the locomotive ran around the train to couple onto the the north end of the train.

The turntable house was circular, and had covered doors on either side to keep winter snow out. The table was swung by manpower, a system not so fondly known as an "Armstrong" turntable.

In March and April of 1899, trains had great difficulty getting through the snow-covered tracks to White Pass; two or three locomotives were needed

The tail of the switchback came to an abrupt end, being just long enough to hold a short train. When a northbound train pulled in from the left track, the switch at the junction was thrown, and the train then backed up the right track. The creek at the photographer's feet is higher than the end of the nearby track.
2710 Yukon Archives/EA Hegg Collection (U. of W.)

After having left the tail of the switchback the train backed across the trestle in the foreground. This trestle is visible in the photograph on the left.
2747 Yukon Archives/EA Hegg Collection (U. of W.)

to haul from three to six heavily-loaded box-cars. Gangs of men shovelled the tracks clear of drifted snow, but even then there were days at a time when trains could not get through. With the coming of spring however, the problem ended. Crews were indeed thankful in 1901 when the great steel cantilever bridge was completed. The bridge joined the old line north of the turntable, and the turntable track then became a seven-car siding.

Above: With throttle at maximum power, the locomotives pound up the 3.8% grade about one-half mile from White Pass summit. The train is led by engines 99, 97, and 93 powered by mighty 800-horsepower, 6-cylinder, Alco diesels. Although famous for making smoke while accelerating or under load, the Alcos are running remarkably clean. In the right foreground can be seen the the original narrow, curving, White Pass Trail.

Below: A morning Summit Excursion is on its way home, having just left White Pass. Engines 93, 94, and 95 tow a string of fifteen cars of mixed age—at the rear is the **Lake Teslin**, built prior to 1926, and ahead of it are four cars built in 1992 and 1993. This area was a welcome sight to those slogging up the "Trail of '98"; the climb was over.

A view overlooking Dead Horse Gulch, the most infamous piece of trail on the route to the Klondike: at the near left can be seen an abandoned WP&YR pump station—behind it was the Switchback turntable; at mid-distance on the left can be seen the Hannan Snow Shed (demolished in 1992); in the distant left are the Sawtooth Mountains; at the upper right is Mine Mountain on whose slopes the Inspiration Point Mine was located—a cableway stretched across the canyon from the mine to the railway grade.

Steel reached White Pass on February 18, 1899. That winter the pass was an important staging point. Material and paid freight were brought this far by rail and forwarded up-line by Heney's Red Line Transportation Company and other teamsters to grading crews and to Bennett. For a short time a small tug and barge worked on five-mile-long Summit Lake, alongside the track at the pass, moving material north to the end of the lake where the wagon road began.

Today, the 1650-foot siding at White Pass is an important piece of track where Summit Excursion trains meet and pass one another. At the peak of the season as many as four trains, in each direction, mornings and afternoons, pass through the gap in the mountains. Although White Pass is referred to as the summit, in fact it is not the highest point on the rail line. Four miles north, near Meadows, the grade crests 75 feet higher.

Flapping in the breeze at the International Boundary, mile 20.4, are the flags of the State of Alaska, the United States, Canada, the Province of British Columbia, and the Yukon. The railway required charters from three different governments before construction of the 110-mile line could begin.

Photo by Mark Baker

Mile 20.9 Canadian Snow Shed site

Just north of the pass was the site of the Canadian Snow Shed, demolished in late 1991. Unlike the Hannan Snow Shed which sheltered track from snow slides, the Canadian and American Snow Sheds provided protection against drifting snow. The shed was not much more than a roof over a long, curving, rock cut.

Here, barely out of the mountains, rail emerges into an open stretch of undulating bedrock cut by ponds, swamps, and circuitous drainage systems—terrain created by the retreat of the last glacier. Heather and sparse stands of stunted alpine fir and juniper dominate the next five miles; flowering plants and alpine meadows (and mosquitoes and black flies); moose and caribou; ptarmigan; beaver ponds and

In 1992, summer came late to White Pass, as evidenced by Summit Lake still frozen over in late June. Engines 94 and 93 have just run around the train of five coaches and are about to return to Skagway.

It is 11:30 a.m. on July 12, 1993, and work extra 108 on the siding at White Pass is being passed by the northbound Fraser turn head-ended by engines 92 and 90. The work train and a track gang are replacing light-weight rail on the siding with heavier rail.

At mile 23.6 the battered remains of snow fences stand on bedrock left barren by the last glacier, as the afternoon Fraser turn blows by. Snow fences reduced the amount of drifting across the tracks. The remains of other snow fences can still be seen along the line.

A Bennett-bound train swings around a disused maintenance-of-way shelter, once a WP&YR box car, at mile 23.8 . Towering on the horizon five miles away is a peak of the Boundary Range, and just beyond it lies Chilkoot Pass

marmot burrows; fox, black bear—yes, and even grizzly bear—patrol this tract in search of food.

When trains operated year-round the stretch between the pass and Fraser could be a nightmare for train crews caught in storms and for rotary snow plow crews attempting to keep the line open.

Mile 23.6 Snow Fence Bald bedrock characterizes much of the wide open landscape where wind-driven snow created hard-packed drifts across the railway tracks. Remnants of the once-important snow fences, feeble attempts to control nature, can still be seen on either side of the tracks at mile 23.6, one of the most exposed sections of track. The open slat-fences created wind eddies, causing snow to be deposited on the lee-side of the fence instead of on the rail grade 200 feet distant.

Mile 25.2, near Meadows, is the highest point on the WP&YR line.

This 1899 Cooke rotary snow plow served for decades on the WP&YR, clearing track from Skagway to Bennett. In the 1960s it was shut down and put on display, first at Bennett, then at Skagway, its snow removal duties taken over by bulldozers. In 1995, the WP&YR began rebuilding the rotary, and in the spring of 1996 it was once again put to work, clearing the higher portions of the rail grade for start-up of the seasonal railway operations. It is seen here just north of White Pass.

photo by Gary Heger/WP&YR

On Bridge 26A over the Thompson River, one mile south of Fraser, locomotives 98 and 90 head for Skagway pulling nine coaches.

An infrequent meet with a work train is seen from the fireman's seat of a 90-class locomotive which is bringing a northbound train into Fraser. The Canada Customs station is to the left, and behind the water tank can be seen a waiting tour bus.

A WP&YR maintenance-of-way track car and trailer rolls through Fraser on the main line. On the far side of the South Klondike Highway are the Canada Customs station, customs officer's residences, and a highway maintenance camp.

Engineer Cliff Fletcher has the southbound Bennett turn moving at an easy fifteen miles per hour at mile 28.1 on the shore of Fraser Lake.

A southbound train has just crossed the bridge over the Thompson River. Bringing up the rear is cupola-outfitted baggage/coach No. 211 and flat car No. 479 which usually has a load of back-packs belonging to returning Chilkoot Pass trekkers.

Mile 24.4   Meadows Like Boulder and Gulch Stations, Meadows is a reference point referred to between dispatchers and train crews.

Mile 24.5 Highest elevation At 2924 feet above sea level, track here is a built-up grade crossing a swampy, stagnant, pond—the highest point on the railway of the WP&YR.

Mile 25.6 At the north end of the marshy area was the original Meadows station, with a short siding which was an important fixture during early operations. Just north of the siding is the "Fraser Hill", the steepest grade (thus the ruling grade, 3.8%) southbound on the line.

In the days of steam, heavy trains, sometimes unable to make the grade, were forced to "double the hill". That is, one-half of the train was cut off at the base of the hill while the locomotive pulled the first half of the train up the hill, on to the siding. The locomotive then backed downgrade to pick up the second half of the train and steamed up to the siding where the train was once more united.

In 1968, the siding was removed, but in winter heavy southbound trains could still encounter trouble; diesel locomotives would slip on snow-covered rail and stall, even with the application of sand. Engineers then had no alternative but to back down towards Fraser and "take a run at the hill".

Mile 26.2 From an alpine landscape, the rail grade now starts to level off into a sub-alpine surrounding. Near the bottom of the steep grade, tracks overlook a small milky-blue lake fed by a waterfall of the Thompson River (as it known by local residents; it is listed on Canadian topographical maps as the Tutshi River.) The colour of the water is due to "glacial flour", fine particles of rock ground from bedrock by slow movement of ice-sheets far up the mountain slopes and carried down by melt-water. Alpine fir stands taller here, and pine makes its appearance; much of the bedrock vanishes under muskeg and meadows, as streams enlarge and merge into ponds, rivers, and lakes.

Above: A special photo-excursion train, returning from Bennett, is seen here passing through Log Cabin, once a very busy spot on the line. Baldwin No. 73 is being assisted by diesels No. 93 and 97.

Opposite: A Bennett excursion train waits while passengers explore what remains of historic Bennett City. For some eighty years travellers were provided with hearty meals at Bennett Station as part of their train ticket.

The only remaining building at Bennett dating from the gold rush days is never-completed St. Andrew's Presbyterian Church. The rail grade, a faint line just above the shoreline, can be seen in the right of the photo.

Mile 26.8 Bridge 26A A low trestle, Bridge 26A, provides the crossing of the Thompson River where the grade is practically level. Previously all-timber, Bridge 26A was shored up with steel pilings in late 1996.

Mile 27.4 Loop track Originally the site of a gravel ballast pit, the flats just south of Fraser were laid with a loop track, all-important for the "rotary fleet" in winter time. Since pusher engines must be behind rotary plows, a wye would have been no use for turning the units when it was heavily snowed-in; the northbound fleet entered the loop and came out

Opposite Top: The WP&YR railway bridge over the Nares River at Carcross was once a swing-bridge to permit passage of steamboats. As such it was seldom used, and was fixed in the closed position and shored up with wooden pilings and steel beams in the 1950s.

Opposite Middle: Parked at Carcross, Yukon, since the 1930s, this 120-year-old Baldwin locomotive is in remarkably good condition. As the **Duchess of Wellington***, it operated between 1878 and the late 1890s at a colliery near Nanaimo, B.C., and between 1900 and 1921 on the Taku Tram, a 3-mile long WP&YR-owned subsidiary tramway, located fifty-five miles south-easterly from Carcross. Originally a 30-inch gauge machine, but converted to 36-inch gauge, the* **Duchess** *never operated on the WP&YR main line.*

Opposite Bottom: Seen at Whitehorse, Yukon, in 1980, locomotive No. 100 displays a short-lived colour scheme used between 1976 and 1980. Only seven of the fleet's nineteen active locomotives got this paint job. Although a very attractive scheme, preparation had been inadequate and the paint deteriorated quickly.

Photo by Robert G. Hilton

Steam locomotive No. 73 does make trips beyond Shops. This special, unscheduled, excursion train was ordered out by WP&YR management to carry a number of photographers. Assisting No. 73 are diesels No. 98 and No. 97, at the falls of the Thompson River, mile 26.2.

of it positioned to plow back southward. Rotaries regularly worked the Alaska section of the track and the section between the pass and Fraser, but occasionally worked all the way to Bennett where there was also a loop track. The Fraser loop was pulled up years ago.

Mile 27.7 Fraser Located here, at an elevation of 2767 feet, are a 2,412-foot siding and a house-track. At trackside stands the railway's last water tank, water spout still in place, sheathed over and painted iron oxide red; it was a most important fixture when steam locomotives ruled the grades. Both coal and water were available at Shops, Glacier, White Pass, Fraser, Bennett, Carcross, Cowley, and Whitehorse; coal was also available at Log Cabin and Pennington—impressive for a line only 110 miles in length.

To the east is alpine Fraser Lake (topographical maps refer to it as Bernard Lake, named after Captain William Moore's son Bernard).

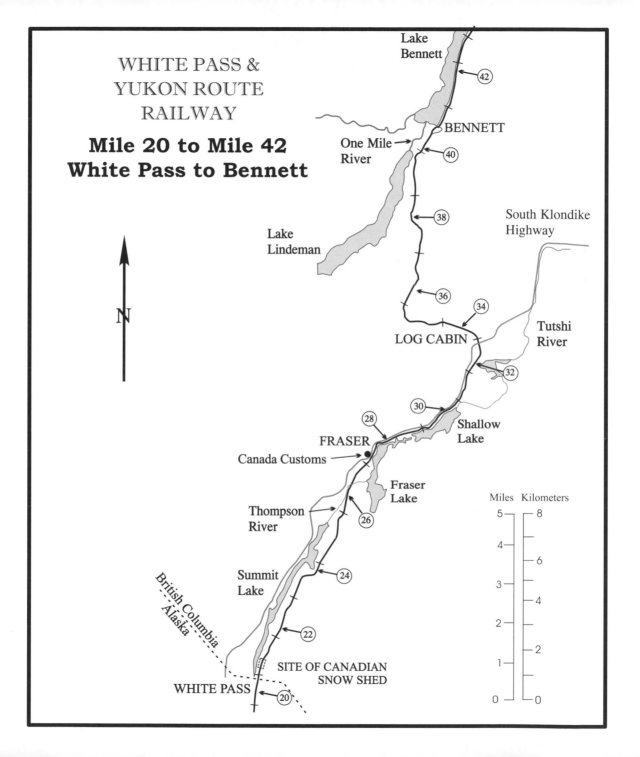

A southbound train leaves Fraser, B.C., located on the shore of Fraser Lake.

At the same location, but ninety-five years earlier, a passenger train leaves Fraser. Leading the train, which consists of a baggage car and five coaches, is WP&YR locomotive No. 53, a Consolidation type built in 1882. Note that the water tank (behind the rearmost coach) was then housed in an octagonal building.

4127 Yukon Archives/MacBride Museum Collection Vol. 2

The South Klondike Highway converges on the railway at Fraser, and a contingent of Canada Customs employees are quartered here to staff the Customs Station which straddles the highway. It is the last settlement on the Canadian side of the International Boundary which is seven miles south. In the peak season a dozen or more buses per day pull through Customs, across the railway, and into the parking lot beside the water tower. Passengers arrive from, and depart for, Skagway by train as a part of package tours of Canada's historic northland. Trains, which lay over here for about a half-hour before heading back south, are part of a scheduled through service—trains frequently run empty, either north or south.

Fraser, B.C., is an important terminus where tour bus passengers transfer to trains. Dominating the station is the water tank, the only one left on the line; the Fraser turn waits as loading takes place.

*In the 1989 to 1992 seasons, the WP&YR operated a track car between Fraser and Bennett to pick up Chilkoot Pass trekkers bound for Skagway, or Fraser. Parks Canada people working out of Bennett also made use of the service. The **Chilkoot Trail Service**, as the track car was known, met both the morning and afternoon Fraser turn, making two runs into Bennett. At the time, the track into Bennett was rough, speed was restricted, and the service was jokingly referred to as the **"Bennett Bullet."** Piloted by Camille Dextraze, the **Bullet** left Carcross (its home base), Yukon, early in the morning and returned home in late afternoon. Seen here, at the north switch at Fraser, the **Bullet** comprises motor car No. 2020 with unpowered trailer No. 2027, and an open trailer. As many as sixteen people could be hauled in the two cars. Trekkers rode the closed cars while their gear tagged along behind. Car 2020 was equipped with a radio and, as the big locomotives, it was in constant contact with the WP&YR dispatcher.*

On a June afternoon, the Bennett turn coasts along Shallow Lake at Portage.

Mile 29.9 Ptarmigan Point After leaving Fraser, trains bound for Bennett and points north wind along the shore of Fraser Lake to reach this rock bluff known as Ptarmigan Point.

Mile 30.4 Portage This is where a small but swift stream joins two lakes. It is a popular fishing spot, and private homes, one fashioned from an old WP&YR boxcar, have been built here.

Mile 32.9 The South Klondike Highway crosses the rail grade at mile 32.9, the last point the railway is accessible by road until Carcross at mile 67.5. A rough parking lot here is available for those hiking the Chilkoot Trail via Bennett and the railway's right-of-way.

Mile 33.0 Log Cabin Log Cabin Station is, at 2,915 feet above sea level, the second highest point on the railway. During the gold rush days of 1898 and 1899, this place was of major importance for those gold-seekers northbound via the White Pass route; here they were monitored by members of a North West Mounted Police detachment and their goods were examined by Canadian Customs officers. It was also a major station on the rail route and a community of services geared to freighters and trekkers.

When news of the Atlin gold strike broke in late July of 1898, many of those bound for the Klondike changed plans, heading back south-easterly via Bennett and the chain of lakes leading down Taku Arm. However, in winter Log Cabin was the jump-off point for two major overland trails to Atlin, much shorter than the route over the chain of frozen lakes. Log Cabin figured in two proposed WP&YR rail extensions: in 1899 towards Atlin and in 1905 towards a gold/silver discovery on Windy Arm; neither got beyond the planning stage.

Today, two rickety shacks at the south end of a 1,656-foot siding are all that remain of the once-active community of Log Cabin.

*The locomotives of the Bennett turn are at the level crossing of the South Klondike Highway, just south of Log Cabin. On the vestibule of car No. 283, **Lake Klukshu**, an intent cameraman is unaware that he also is being photographed. To the left is the railway's long-abandoned telephone line, and the not-so-long-abandoned fuel oil pipeline.*

Mile 37.8 To the south of Log Cabin all streams drain into the Tutshi River, eventually to reach Taku Arm (which flows into Tagish Lake); to the north water flows into Lake Bennett which then flows into Tagish Lake via Nares Lake at Carcross. In a low, interior, mountain pass, Log Cabin lies on swampy, flat, ground with sluggish drainage. Vegetation here is fairly lush with thick stands of pine. As the terrain slopes away, northward, streams gain size and velocity, and lakes make their appearance. Such is Beaver Lake which comes into view at mile 37.8.

Mile 40.0 This steep stretch of track has a 3.3% grade. Through breaks in the trees, Lake Lindeman (frequently misspelled Linderman) can be spotted at mile 40.0; above Lake Bennett and connected to it by a short, turbulent, and swift stream, Lake Lindeman was considered the head of navigation— at least for small craft—on the route to the Klondike via Chilkoot Pass.

Mile 40.6   Bennett Bennett Station lies on the shore of Lake Bennett, 2,156 feet above sea level. On July 6, 1899, the last rail between Skagway and Bennett was spiked down. As important as this event was, Lake Bennett had already seen a lot of history. For generations Chilkat Indians had used Chilkoot Pass and Lake Bennett to reach the interior, and Europeans had begun using this same route to the Upper Yukon River as early as 1882— all part of a wave of gold prospecting which had swept up the west coast of North America, beginning with the California gold rush of 1849.

Every year until the early summer of 1897, there had been a small but significant stream of hardy men heading for "the Yukon" in search of gold, and many made it pay. To them Lake Bennett was known as "Boat Lake". Then, when word of the great Klondike strike reached southern cities in July of 1897 (the discovery was actually made in August of 1896) near madness prevailed. The rush of '98 is the stuff of legends. About thirty thousand came over in the winter of 1897-98, but most arrived at

The Bennett turn has just arrived at Bennett. Chilkoot Pass hikers outbound from Bennett have already begun stowing their pack gear on the flat car, and a passenger who has just arrived on the train is disembarking for a half-hour jaunt about the historic site.

Lake Bennett in early spring of 1898. More than seven thousand boats were slapped together on the shores of Lakes Lindeman and Bennett, and with the break-up of ice on May 29, 1898, the armada set off. Ho for the Klondike!

That spring several small steamers were built on both Lake Lindeman and Lake Bennett; material had been dragged over the Chilkoot Pass.

Thousands of tons of freight, and passengers, rode the steamers to the head of Miles Canyon just above Whitehorse, where other transportation companies carried on. In 1899 a number of more substantial steamers, brought knocked-down over White and Chilkoot Passes, were assembled at Bennett. It was a boom town complete with most amenities, and was a very important shipping port. More steamers were built at Bennett in 1900, but its days as a port were numbered—the whole rail line

Engine No. 67 was built by Baldwin for the WP&YR in 1901 and retired in 1951. The train is stopped at Bennett for the traditional "free" meal provided its passengers here. The station, shown in its modern form on page 41, has changed very little.

to Whitehorse was complete in late July, and steamboat traffic almost instantly ceased on Lake Bennett. After only two summers and a couple of months, the slap of paddle wheels could no longer be heard on the lake.

Today, Bennett consists of the White Pass' station building, a few other structures, and high on the pine-covered ridge overlooking Lake Bennett the skeleton of St. Andrew's Presbyterian Church. Started by Klondikers, but never completed, the church is the only remains of the original village which was strung out for a half-mile along the shore of Lake Bennett. Bennett has a 3,960 foot siding, a yard, and a loop track (originally for turning snow plows). For twenty-seven miles northerly the rail line follows the shore of the lake before reaching Carcross.

Mile 46.6 Pavey Station, now abandoned.

Mile 49.3   Heney/Graves This was Heney Station from 1972 until 1988. In 1989 it became Graves Station, as it is currently listed, with a siding 2,154 feet in length.

Mile 50.6   A one-mile section along the lake in this vicinity required very heavy rock-work, and was said to have cost $250,000—the most expensive mile on the whole line.

Mile 51.6 Pennington Station was once the site of a railway maintenance gang, and a short siding once existed here.

Mile 52.6 BC - Yukon Border One mile north of Pennington the railway crosses into the Yukon from British Columbia.

The WP&YR railway swing bridge over the Nares River at Carcross in 1944. The bridge could be swung open, pivoting at the centre, to permit passage of steamboats. The view is to the south, looking towards Lake Bennett, and the railway's water tank at the end of the bridge is a prominent feature.
Photo by Ron W. Willis

Mile 55.6 Pit A short spur known as Pit.

Mile 59.6 Watson Station, Yukon, also on the shore of Lake Bennett, is the site of a 1,656-foot siding.

Mile 67.5 Carcross Carcross village, originally named Caribou Crossing, was for a short time simply Caribou, but was changed since a number of other "Caribous" then existed in the North. At 2,161 feet above sea level, the village is located at the foot of Lake Bennett where the short Nares River drains the lake. The railway crosses Nares River over what was originally a swing bridge which permitted sternwheelers to pass from Lake Bennett into Nares Lake. When the railway was completed there was little further need for steamers on the waterway so the swing bridge was later fixed permanently closed and supported by

pilings. The "last spike" marking completion of the 110-mile railway was driven here at Carcross, on July 29, 1900.

Before the completion of the South Klondike Highway in the 1980s, a Canadian Customs Office was located at Carcross since, other than railway maintenance camps down the line, it was the closest Canadian community to the International Boundary. American tourists, just off the train and bound for a cruise on the lakes to the south, had to pass through the Customs Office at Carcross. Steamboats had been making this voyage since the Atlin gold strike of 1898, but in the fall of 1955 the White Pass shut down its river division and the **Tutshi**, the last sternwheeler on the "Southern Lakes", was hauled onto the ways at Carcross.

On the Nares River is the old steamer dock at Carcross, with the WP&YR station behind. Passengers from Skagway could detrain at the station and walk onto the adjoining dock to take a steamer down Taku Arm. The barge and boat seen in the foreground of the photo opposite are moored at this same dock.

*The new 32-passenger rail bus purchased by the WP&YR specially for service between Fraser, B.C., and Carcross, Yukon, is pictured at the railway station in Carcross. It is named the **Red Line**, after railway contractor Heney's Red Line Transportation Company. Although still WP&YR property, the station is now the home of the Carcross Visitor's Centre.*

From a painting by J. Craig Thorpe/WP&YR

No trains had run through Carcross since October 1982, but in September of 1988 a work train made its way northward over deteriorated trackage to retrieve two locomotives and a number of freight cars which had been left in Whitehorse. Not until early summer of 1997 did another locomotive make Carcross, leading a work train which went about reinforcing the bridge over the Nares River. This was in preparation for a reenactment of the shipping of the "Ton of Gold", an event of July, 1897 which triggered the world's greatest gold rush. On July 12, 1997, the first passenger train in almost fifteen years entered Carcross. Later that fall a special train made its way over rough trackage to reach Whitehorse—an event to cheer White Pass fans around the world.

Scheduled trains had run only as far as Bennett prior to 1997, but for the 1998 season the White Pass acquired a self-propelled rail car to make regular trips between Fraser and Carcross.

A track maintenance crew, working the active line north of the International Boundary, operates out of Carcross. Although in rough shape, a wye and a 2,340-foot siding at Carcross are still serviceable.

North of Carcross, track is intact although in poor condition. Several stations existed at one time or another along the 43-mile stretch to Whitehorse, some abandoned long ago.

Mile 74.9   Lansdowne Station: elevation 2,357 feet.

Mile 79.4   Lorne Station at 2,356 feet has an 1,836-foot siding.

Mile 81.5   Minto Station: elevation 2,416 feet.

Mile 89.0   Robinson Station at 2,507 feet is at a minor summit.

Mile 95.5   Cowley Station, at elevation 2,463 feet was once home to a track maintenance crew. One decrepit building and an 828-foot siding are still in place here.

The siding at Cowley, Yukon, has suffered from heaving by permafrost. This track last saw scheduled traffic in October of 1982. Exactly six years later, a work train did make its way from Skagway, through Cowley, to Whitehorse to retrieve rolling stock.

Mile 104.0 Macrae Station at 2,397 feet elevation was located at the rail crossing of the Alaska Highway, and at one time was a junction when the Pueblo Spur was added. The station was revived in 1969 when the WP&YR began shipping lead/zinc concentrates from the giant Cyprus Anvil mine at Faro, Yukon. Concentrate hoppers were transferred from trucks and loaded on special flat cars here.

Mile 105.5 Utah Station is a large yard just off the Alaska Highway which came into being during WW II, serving general contractor Utah Construction. The yard was later used to store the cars which carried Anvil mine concentrates from Macrae to Skagway.

Mile 106.0 Canyon Former Canyon Station, at elevation 2,373 feet, was located just above the foot bridge crossing Miles Canyon.

Mile 110.7 Whitehorse At the end of steel, Whitehorse lies at 2,083 feet above sea level. The settlement began life as a camp at the foot of Miles Canyon and the Whitehorse Rapids, where Klondikers either portaged gear around the rapids or shot the rapids—as many Bennett-built steamboats did. For fifty-seven years Whitehorse was the head of Yukon River navigation and home port for most of the WP&YR's steamer fleet.

Initially, the WP&YR had not been in the commercial riverboat business, but in January, 1900, the company bought the Canadian Development Company which had the largest fleet of steam-powered sternwheelers operating on the upper Yukon River. Within three years the WP&YR also bought up other shipping companies to gain a virtual monopoly on traffic from Skagway to Dawson City. Departing Whitehorse, steamers took two days to reach the Klondike, but the return trip, upstream, took as many as five days. The summer shipping season on the river was a short five months long.

During the four-week fall freeze-up and spring break-up there could be little traffic. In winter, however, the WP&YR continued to operate the stage service organized by the Canadian Development Company. Horse-drawn sleighs carried light express and passengers on the 325-mile route, stopping at road houses and stables situated twenty to twenty-five miles apart. There, passengers ate and slept, and horses rested and were fed. In 1922 the WP&YR sold the winter stage service to a private operator.

In addition to the large rail yard and maintenance centre at Whitehorse, the WP&YR also had a ship-building yard staffed with skilled shipwrights who built steamboats, gas boats, and barges. On the bank of the Yukon River all craft were hauled up on the "ways" in fall for annual maintenance, and re-launched next spring. The shipyards ceased to function in the fall of 1955 when the WP&YR's last two sternwheelers on the upper Yukon River were permanently shut down (coincidental with the opening of a highway between Whitehorse and Dawson City). Today only two sternwheelers remain: the **Klondike** which is on display in Whitehorse, and the **Keno** in Dawson City—both were built in the WP&YR's Whitehorse shipyard.

From 1900 until World War II, the population of Whitehorse averaged slightly more than 500. The numbers swelled to 20,000 in 1943 when the U.S. military and Alcan construction crews flooded Whitehorse, but by 1946 the population fell practically to pre-war levels. However, Yukon development then began, and the population rose—steadily—from 2500 in 1950 to 10,000 in 1970, to its present 18,000.

Whitehorse became the capital of the Yukon in 1955, supplanting Dawson as the Territory's administrative centre. Although quiet in the winter months, the city bustles with the coming of spring and the very important tourism industry. While the closure of WP&YR rail operations in 1982 did hurt the Yukon's economy, recovery was not far behind; even during the gold boom days of 1898-1900, Whitehorse did not experience such activity as can be seen today.

Following shutdown of the railway in 1982, the WP&YR station in Whitehorse was used as a company administration building until the mid-1990s when it was vacated and locked up.

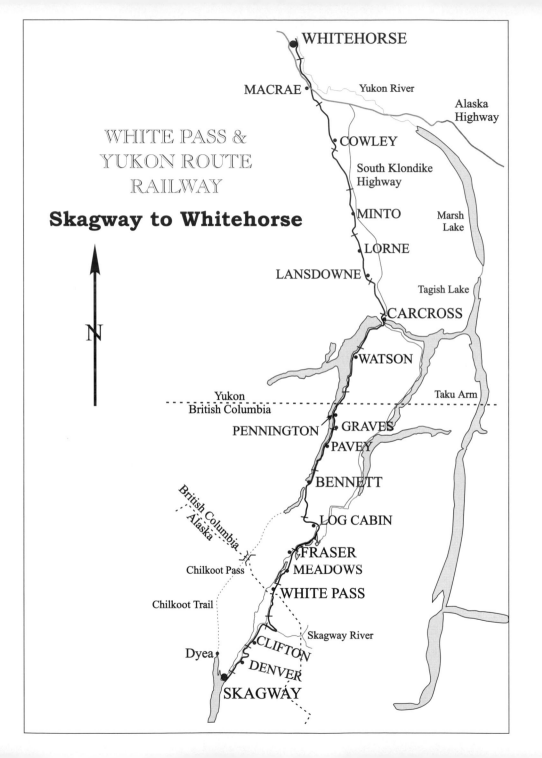

THE STORY OF THE
WHITE PASS & YUKON ROUTE

1896 to 1898

GOLD -
THE RUSH TO THE KLONDIKE

Gold was discovered in August of 1896 on a relatively inaccessible creek in the Yukon District of the North-West Territories, and the new gold-field was soon christened "the Klondike". Men had been scouring the creeks along the Yukon River since the early 1880s, and had already established several good workings prior to 1896. The news of George Washington Carmacks' great Klondike strike burst on west coast cities in July of 1897, creating a state of near-madness. Promoters and entrepreneurs, con men, rich men and the unemployed poor, all swarmed to the ports of San Francisco, Portland, Seattle, Victoria, and Vancouver. The world was in the depths of a recession which, until then, had offered little hope for most. Gold, all imagined, was the realization of an incredible dream.

At the time of the great find there were only two developed routes into the Klondike. The favoured approach was by way of Chilkoot Pass, the other by way of the lower Yukon River. By either, the journey from "civilization" to the Klondike was expensive and time-consuming. Northbound miners and prospectors left Pacific coast ports of the United States or south-western British Columbia in late winter or early spring to reach the Yukon in a month, or more. The veteran Yukoners were known as sourdoughs, the novices as cheechakos.

Most (about nine out of ten) began by taking a week-long, 1000-mile, passage by commercial coastal steamer from Seattle, Washington, or Victoria, British Columbia, to Juneau and on to Dyea, Alaska. Dumped off there, at the mouth of the Taiya River, they were on their own, taking several weeks to pack tons of supplies up the Taiya River, over still-frozen Chilkoot Pass into north-western British Columbia. The route had been pioneered centuries before by the Chilkat Indians

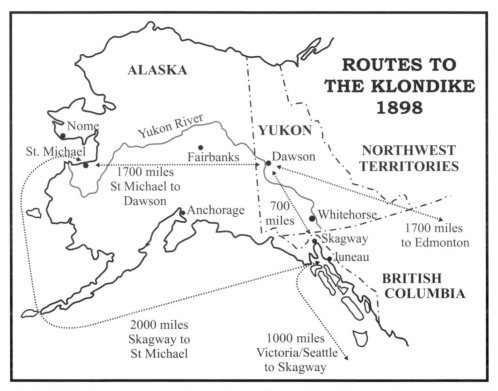

ROUTES TO
THE KLONDIKE
1898

ALASKA

NORTHWEST
TERRITORIES

YUKON

Nome

Yukon River

St. Michael

Fairbanks

Dawson

1700 miles
St Michael to
Dawson

Anchorage

700
miles

Whitehorse

1700 miles
to Edmonton

Skagway

Juneau

BRITISH
COLUMBIA

2000 miles
Skagway to
St Michael

1000 miles
Victoria/Seattle
to Skagway

who were in the 1890s still using it to trade with the interior "Stick" Indians. Descending the east side of the pass, to Lake Bennett, stampeders spent another few weeks whip-sawing lumber for construction of boats. When the ice broke up in late May, men were on their way, rowing or sailing along a string of lakes and streams—and rapids—which led to the upper Yukon River. The six hundred miles of waterways between Lake Bennett and Dawson City took the better part of two weeks of travel.

The optional, all-water, route to the Klondike involved a 3000-mile steamer voyage from Victoria or Seattle to St. Michael near the mouth of the Yukon River. There on the west coast of Alaska, trading companies had been operating stern-wheeled steamboats well up the Yukon River since 1869. Unable to set off until late May when ice on the frozen rivers finally broke up, the steamers churned 1700 miles up the Yukon River, through north-central Alaska, reaching the Klondike District in early June. By either this or the Chilkoot route, men could prospect and work placer claims for five or six months before winter once more ruled the Yukon, freezing up mine workings and waterways, and cutting off transport of any volume of freight and supplies until next spring.

Formerly a part of Canada's North-West Territories, the Yukon Territory came into being in 1898; prior to that the Yukon District was only a general area comprising the watershed of the upper half of the great river. At Dawson City, where the population rocketed to over 30,000 by 1899, an efficient freight transportation system was desperately needed. A number of giant sternwheelers were built in 1897 and 1898 specially for use on the lower Yukon River between St. Michael, Alaska, and Dawson, but this was still the expensive route. At the same time, the shorter, "poor man's", route over Chilkoot Pass soon saw development in the form of organized freighting to the base of the pass, cable tramlines over the hump, and ferrying to Lake Bennett. A boat- and ship-building industry developed at Bennett, and a number of smaller steamboats were built there (most were prefabricated elsewhere and knocked down for shipment over the passes), some for use on the Southern Lakes (Bennett to Miles Canyon, and on Taku Arm), and others destined for use on the upper Yukon River between Whitehorse and Dawson. A horse-powered tramway got men and freight around treacherous waters of Miles Canyon and Whitehorse Rapids through which steamboats were able to descend, but not ascend. From Whitehorse, at the foot of the rapids, it was almost clear sailing down-river to Dawson.

Captain William Moore had staked out land at the mouth of the Skagway River in 1887 when the only practical route through the mountains to the interior was over Chilkoot Pass via nearby Dyea; he had just learned of the little-known White Pass from the Chilkat Indians. After hacking out a rough trail to the summit he was convinced the route would one day be the scene of rail traffic to the as yet uncharted Upper Yukon District, and that his land (now Skagway) would be an important salt-water port. How right he was!

Parallel to Chilkoot Pass and only six miles southerly, White Pass was a more difficult packing route, but because of its topography there was better potential for construction of a wagon road or a railway. As transportation mechanisms over Chilkoot Pass were being put into place, work also began on Brackett's wagon road from Skagway, over White Pass, and on to Lake Bennett where it merged with the Chilkoot route. Transportation over the 100-odd miles from Skagway or Dyea to Whitehorse would become a nightmare of obstacles, congestion, and despair. Speculators saw a railway as the only realistic alternative.

Many locations had their names or spelling changed during the gold rush years.

First spelled Skagua, then Skaguay, the village is now officially known as Skagway. Similarly, Whitehorse was first known as White Horse, then for a brief time as Closeleigh. Even Canada's Northwest Territories was first named North-West Territories.

1898 to 1900

CONSTRUCTION - STEEL OVER WHITE PASS

Transportation to the new goldfield was an enormous problem, and the only practical year-round means of passage over the coastal mountains to central Yukon was—as Moore had prophesied—soon determined to be a railway over White Pass. A syndicate of London, England, investors (the firm of Close Brothers and Company) had acquired charters for a railway over the pass, without knowing whether or not a practical route could be found.

First surveyors of the route had concluded construction of a rail grade would be nigh unto impossible. But on his own initiative, Irish-Canadian Michael J. Heney, a temporarily unemployed railway contractor, had by early April of 1898 personally scouted a feasible line from Skagway to Lake Bennett. In a chance meeting in a Skagway hotel soon after, Heney conferred with three representatives of the English backers of the syndicate. An all-night session convinced civil engineers Erastus C. Hawkins, an American, Sir Thomas Tancred, an Englishman, and John Hislop, a Canadian, that steel could be laid over White Pass.

And so it was. Word reached London and firm plans were laid. Close Brother would finance the whole project—unlike most other railways built through Canadian territory at the time, the WP&YR received

---

*Unemployment wasn't always a problem. On July 1, 1898, Michael Heney made this offer in the **Seattle Daily Times.***

Assembled on the shore of Lake Bennett in 1899 is part of Michael Heney's construction crews and his Red Line Transportation fleet— note the row of wagons lined up on the right side of the track. Seated on a horse in the foreground is Heney himself. This site will become Bennett Station. Of particular interest is the sternwheeler **Olive May**, *seen on the left. It was one of a dozen small steamers whose components were packed over the passes in early 1898 for assembly on Lake Bennett and Lake Lindeman where they served as interim transportation for more than two seasons. The* **Olive May** *operated later on the Yukon River and Lake Laberge, and sank and was raised several times in its short career—it is believed to have been the inspiration for the steamer* **Alice May** *in Robert Service's poem, The Cremation of Sam McGee.*

no federal assistance. Not much more than a month later, on May 27, 1898, construction of the rail line began with Heney the chief contractor, and Hawkins as the general manager. The plan included a railway from Skagway, over White Pass, on to Lake Bennett, and terminating at the village of Whitehorse, at the foot of the Whitehorse Rapids. An extension from Whitehorse, to Fort Selkirk, 300 miles northerly, was planned but never built.

DO NOT BE MISLED

*When the tracks reached Lake Bennett, the WP&YR boasted about its new shipping capability in the August 6, 1899 issue of Victoria's **Daily Colonist**. Note that Skagway is spelled two ways in the ad.*

Passing through three territories, the rail system required charters from three different governments:

Pacific and Arctic Railway and Navigation Company, from the United States

British Columbia-Yukon Railway Company, from the Province of British Columbia

British Yukon Mining, Trading and Transportation Company, from the Government of Canada,

In 1900 the name of the latter company was changed to simply the **British Yukon Railway Company**. All charters had been sanctioned in 1897. In 1901 the **British Yukon Navigation Company** was organized to operate the company's steamboat fleet. All four concerns would operate under the **White Pass and Yukon Railway Company**, a holding company chartered in England. The company's whole transportation system was given the "umbrella" name of the **White Pass and Yukon Route**—abbreviated to the "WP&YR"—to describe service from Skagway to destinations in Alaska, British Columbia, and the Yukon Territory. The acronym, WP&YR, is still very well known today.

The railway grade would rise on average about 65 feet per mile in the first five miles, and then average about 180 feet gain in elevation per mile in the next fifteen miles where White Pass was attained at 2,885 feet above sea level. Governing the tonnage which can be hauled over a particular stretch of track is the "ruling grade", that is the steepest piece of track at some point, or points, along the line. The ruling grade northward would be 3.8%, or a rise of 3-8/10 feet for every 100 feet

of track—in downtown Skagway the grade is practically 0%. From the pass northward there would be short stretches of steep up-and-down grades, but overall a drop in elevation of only 800 hundred feet in the ninety miles between White Pass and Whitehorse.

Needless to say, difficulties at times seemed impossible to overcome: the terrain, the weather, the manpower problem, government inaction, legalities, competition from other transportation companies, and minimal financing. But, rails were in place at White Pass by February 22 of 1899, and reached Bennett, at mile 41, on July 25. Using steamers and barges on Lake Bennett, men and materials were moved up to Carcross where surveys and clearing on the 43-mile section between Carcross and Whitehorse had already begun. This section was completed on July 8, 1900, and the 27-mile section along Lake Bennett, between Bennett and Carcross, was completed on July 29, 1900, to open the whole line to train traffic.

During construction of the line, the WP&YR had bought out the Chilkoot Pass tramway companies, the Miles Canyon Tramway, and Brackett's wagon road (White Pass toll road), all of which in July of 1900 became obsolete anyway. In the early 1900s, the WP&YR bought up most of the steamboat companies operating on the Yukon River and on the Upper Lakes, to control traffic into both the Atlin goldfield and the great Klondike goldfield—the company held a near monopoly.

1901 to 1917

THRIVING BUSINESS - HEADY DAYS

During the summer seasons of the first seventeen years of operation, the WP&YR had fairly good business, generating dividends for shareholders. On the other hand, winter operation was decidedly quiet, with a modest but steady stream of passenger traffic utilizing trains to Whitehorse, and a winter stage transfer to Dawson. The population of the Yukon Territory fell from a high of more than 30,000 in 1898, to 27,000 in 1901, to 8,000 in 1911, and to 4,000 in 1921. World War I had drawn men from the Klondike and adversely affected gold production there.

In the early 1900s, a northbound special excursion train has stopped at White Pass Station right on the Alaska/British Columbia boundary. This train is made up of only the locomotive and tender, two coaches, and an "open-air observation car" rigged up from a flat car.
5477 Yukon Archives/H.C. Barley Collection Vol. 3.

THE MEADOWS.B.C.

H.C.BARLE

In 1899 or 1900, a heavy southbound train steams through *"THE MEADOWS, B.C."* at about mile 25, the highest point on the railway's line. Note that a second locomotive is cut in behind the fourth box car, possibly to assist in the pull up the steepest grade (3.8%) on the Canadian side of the boundary, less than a mile behind the train. In the lead is locomotive No. 7, later renumbered to 57, built by Baldwin in 1899 for the WP&YR; in 1906 it was sold to the Klondike Mines Railway which began operations out of Dawson City, Yukon Territory, that year.

5508 Yukon Archives/H.C. Barley Collection Vol. 3.

Although varying from year to year, freight tonnages averaged 35,000 tons annually, for example: 38,000 tons in 1901, 32,000 tons in 1908, and 37,000 tons in 1916. Copper mines served by the WP&YR's 10.8-mile Pueblo spur, built northerly from Macrae Junction in 1911, supplied the bulk of the tonnage between 1912 and 1917. The number of passengers carried slowly declined from 18,000 in 1901 to 8,000 in 1916, but passenger revenue had not so much effect on total revenue as did freight. With reductions in freight rates, net operating revenue of the railway declined by about 45% from 1901 to 1917 in spite of the relatively steady traffic. After 1917, net revenue declined significantly, and no recovery was seen until the 1940s.

In 1901, the railway's first full operating season, the WP&YR had eighteen locomotives on hand. Eight had been bought new, and the rest were small, aging, machines not suitable for mainline service. By 1906 the WP&YR had sold off No. 57 which had been purchased new in 1899, and five of its old, light-weight, locomotives leaving only twelve others on the property. However, two more new locomotives were purchased in 1907 and in 1908; no more were acquired until 1938. The railway had begun business in 1900 with eight passenger cars and 150 freight cars; by 1917 these numbers had increased to eighteen and 201.

Until the mid-1940s, WP&YR tracks ran down the centre of Broadway which today is still Skagway's main thoroughfare. Behind the locomotive, on the track curving to the left, is a coach parked in front of the railway station; between the locomotive and coach, docks can be seen in the distance. Except for being paved with asphalt now, Broadway has not changed much.

*Vancouver Public Library
Photograph Number 9779*

1918 to 1941

RECESSION -
THE RAILWAY PLUGS AWAY

A concerted effort by the WP&YR to attract tourists resulted in a rise from a low of 7,000 passengers carried per year in 1918 to an average of 15,000 between 1925 and 1942—in spite of two bad seasons, 1932 and 1933, when only 6,000 per year came North. Most of the summer-only travellers were brought by coastal steamship lines which made Skagway a port of call. The WP&YR actively promoted tourism, and supplied tourist agencies with attractive promotional literature. In 1917, the WP&YR built the 1041-ton steamer **Tutshi** for voyages on Taku Arm, the 286-ton motor vessel **Tarahne** for Atlin Lake, and the Atlin Inn, to open a wonderful wilderness paradise to Southerners on vacation. Similarly, WP&YR steamboats on the upper Yukon River catered to those wanting a look at the North and the fabled Klondike.

Passenger traffic fluctuated, but annual freight tonnage remained low after the 81,000-ton high of 1917. Tonnage ranged from only 10,000 to 25,000 annually between 1918 and 1942. Mining in the Yukon went into dormancy in the 1930s, not to be revived until the 1950s. The exception was, of course, the Yukon Consolidated Gold Corporation whose dredging operations in the Klondike continued to grind steadily away until 1966. Still,

there was the annual demand for living necessities of Yukon communities and supplies for mining companies, although the gold boom days were over.

As an indication of the static business levels during the slack years, the WP&YR acquired no locomotives between 1908 and 1938 when the company had only eight still in active service. The last to be purchased was No. 69, a Consolidation built by the Baldwin Locomotive Works for the company in June of 1908. In 1938 the company bought a Mikado, No. 70, built by Baldwin in May of that year specially for the WP&YR. Another identical locomotive, No. 71, was built for the railway in 1939. The railway now had twenty-five passenger cars and 192 freight cars.

Although good passenger traffic had been sustained through the early 1930s, all-important freight traffic was too low to provide more than marginal net revenue. In the early 1940s it was not good times but a grim, world-wide, conflict that brought the WP&YR back to rosy-cheeked health, at least for a five-year period.

1942 to 1945

WORLD WAR II -
A MIGHTY RESURGENCE

Fear of a Japanese invasion of the west coast of North America in the darkest days of World War II mobilized the enormous Alcan (Alaska-Canada) Highway project, now known as the Alaska Highway: a 1,523-mile road stretching between Dawson Creek, British Columbia, and Fairbanks, Alaska. (Dawson Creek was the terminus of the Northern Alberta Railways, and the southernmost staging point for highway construction.) This would finally yield an overland link between the southern forty-eight states, through Alberta, British Columbia, and the Yukon Territory, to Alaska. Already in place at the time of construction start-up in early 1942 were a string of airfields, from Grande Prairie to Whitehorse, which would become part of the United States' North West Staging Route to Fairbanks, and on to the USSR. In conjunction with the highway project, work began simultaneously on the Canol (Canadian Oil) Project: development of an oil field in the Northwest Territories, four pipe-lines, and a refinery at Whitehorse. The Canol Project was to have made the North self-sufficient for petroleum products. In charge of the projects was the US Army.

Now, more than forty years after the great Klondike gold rush, there still remained only two practical routes into the Yukon, and the only one with any year-round capability of supplying construction camps was that of the WP&YR. However, the railway was not equipped to handle the volume of freight demanded by the Alcan and Canol projects. On October 1, 1942, the U.S. Army leased the railway and brought in seventeen used locomotives, eleven new locomotives, and a number of freight cars to handle once-more booming traffic to Whitehorse. The civilian employees were retained, but they were overwhelmed by almost three times their number in military employees. In early 1942 the WP&YR had run as few as two trains per week, but during the peak of the Alcan construction days as many as seventeen trains operated in a day, and freight hauled approached 300,000 tons annually.

Earth-moving equipment used in upgrading the Alcan Highway is seen on WP&YR flat cars on the Whitehorse waterfront in summer of 1943, viewed from the upper deck of the sternwheeler **Whitehorse**. *The town is alive with activity, the population having increased 40-fold with the arrival of the massive workforce.*
Photo by Ron W. Willis

1946 to 1953

PEACETIME - DOLDRUMS

In 1946, the U.S. Army cancelled the WP&YR lease, turning operations back to the owners. The military had made many improvements to the railway: relocation of track in Skagway, new equipment, and new facilities. However, in the fever of Alcan activities, maintenance had been deferred, and the WP&YR now had a line in need of major work. What was worse though, was that business was once more down to pre-war levels.

Most of the locomotives brought to Skagway by the U.S. Army were sent back south for scrapping in 1946, but a few were left with the WP&YR. In 1947 the WP&YR placed its last order for steam locomotives. Like No. 70 and No. 71, the new locomotives numbered 72 and 73 were also Mikados built by Baldwin. On arrival of the new units, the WP&YR still had about a dozen locomotives on the active list. At this time there were twenty-five passenger cars and 196 freight cars on the property.

The Alaska Highway as completed in November of 1942 was of no use for commercial traffic—in fact it was no more than a "Cat" road in need of massive up-grading. Contractors finished building the road to standards in 1943, and following the war, the highway was turned over to the Canadian Army for control and maintenance. But post-war traffic was initially very light, being restricted by the military. The road was not immediately competitive with the railway of the WP&YR, since truck freighting over the road could not be done reliably year-round.

However, as the highway was improved, and as commercial truck lines were established, rail traffic suffered. In 1948 the WP&YR itself formed a bus line operating under its British Yukon Navigation Company (under which the river steamers also operated). The company also established its own trucking line, operating between Dawson Creek, B.C., and Whitehorse. Additionally, the U.S. military had upgraded airfields across northern Alberta, British Columbia, and the Yukon Territory, for use by newer and much larger aircraft. Post-war commercial air lines took away much of the passenger traffic formerly handled by coastal ships and the railway. So, once more the railway of the WP&YR found itself in difficulties.

In 1951 the White Pass and Yukon Corporation, a brand-new concern founded in Winnipeg, was granted a charter by the Government of Canada to acquire the four operating companies of the WP&YR which up until then had been owned by the British shareholders of the White Pass and Yukon Railway Company. On November 1 of that year the new business was operational, and began making plans to exploit the inevitable reawakening of the Yukon Territory to mining and tourism.

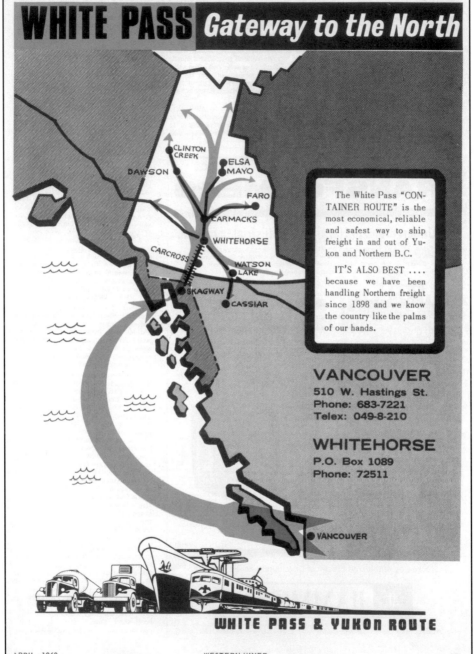

WHITE PASS *Gateway to the North*

The White Pass "CONTAINER ROUTE" is the most economical, reliable and safest way to ship freight in and out of Yukon and Northern B.C.

IT'S ALSO BEST .... because we have been handling Northern freight since 1898 and we know the country like the palms of our hands.

VANCOUVER
510 W. Hastings St.
Phone: 683-7221
Telex: 049-8-210

WHITEHORSE
P.O. Box 1089
Phone: 72511

WHITE PASS & YUKON ROUTE

1954 to 1982

REJUVENATION -
YUKON REVIVAL, AND SLUMP

The steam-propulsion era in the Yukon Territory was coming to an end. An all-weather road was completed between Whitehorse and Dawson in 1955, and the two remaining WP&YR steamboats on the upper Yukon River, the **Klondike** and the **Keno**, ceased operating that year. On the Southern Lakes, the steamboat **Tutshi** also carried its final passengers in 1955. Although eight steam locomotives were still in use in 1954, the WP&YR placed its first order for a pair of relatively small, 84-ton, 800-horsepower, General Electric diesel-electric road locomotives in that year. This was the first obvious sign of modernization of the WP&YR. It has been said that the railway in fact wanted steam locomotives, but could find no builders to construct a small order of narrow gauge machines.

The WP&YR then introduced the first ship-train-truck containerization scheme in the world. The company already had a thriving highway freight truck line serving the central Yukon, and in 1955 launched the first ship in the world designed for container haulage. Although the containers, at 8x8x7 feet, were small by today's standards, the system would later become the major means of international shipping around the globe. The Yukon was now coming to life, with several mining projects maturing. In special containers, products of the mines, silver-lead-zinc concentrate and

asbestos, were moved by WP&YR trucks to Whitehorse where they were shipped by rail to Skagway, and out to processors. Still an isolated ocean port, Skagway was not accessible by a highway until 1978.

Between 1956 and 1963, the WP&YR bought nine more General Electric locomotives, almost identical to those two bought in 1954. Following the arrival of the last engines, all of the steam locomotives except numbers 72 and 73 were retired, and this pair was side-lined in 1964. No. 72 was burned badly in the roundhouse fire of 1969, and was later sold to a southern tourist railway for spare parts. No. 73, in storage for some years, was later restored. The eleven diesels numbered 90 to 100 became the WP&YR's motive power.

The 1960s saw a further rise in Yukon mining activity, demanding greater freight hauling capacity on the railway. In 1969 the WP&YR took delivery of seven bigger, 136-ton, 1200-horsepower engines built by the Montreal Locomotive Works; they were numbered 101 to 107. In a disastrous round-house fire in late 1969, locomotives No. 102 and No. 105, less than six months old, were destroyed. In 1971, the WP&YR bought three new identical locomotives, numbered 108 to 110, to replace those lost in the fire.

---

*In **Western Miner** magazine, the WP&YR advertised its intermodal shipping to the North in 1969.*

These latest locomotives had been purchased to meet a contract for hauling concentrates produced by a new, giant, open pit mine just being developed at Faro, north-westerly from Whitehorse. The Anvil Mining Corporation, Limited (in 1974 the company name was changed to Cyprus Anvil Mining Corporation, Limited), had lead/zinc/silver ore reserves which forecast a mine life of more than twenty years. In 1970 the mill at Faro was started up, and WP&YR trucks began moving concentrates to a loading facility at Macrae Station, on the main line just south of Whitehorse. Special containers and flat cars to carry concentrates were built for the railway. At Skagway, a container dumping facility, storage bins, and ship-loading mechanisms had already been built. The railway's future was bright indeed, as something like 400,000 to 500,000 tons of concentrate per year were forecast for shipment.

In early 1973, Federal Industries Limited, a Canadian company with origins dating back to 1929, bought 50.2% of the common shares of the White Pass and Yukon Corporation, and in 1976 acquired the remaining shares.

Business boomed during the 1970s, but a world-wide recession was in the offing. Metal prices dropped and as a consequence the Cyprus Anvil mine and concentrator at Faro were shut down on June 4, 1982. Cyprus Anvil had become the railway's major shipper, and without its business the WP&YR had no option but to suspend railway operations on October 8, 1982. The sudden loss of traffic had not been anticipated. To meet projected traffic demands the WP&YR had already ordered four more 1200-horsepower locomotives from Bombardier, Inc. (successor to Montreal

*In the early 1900s, a short mixed train pauses and passengers alight for the photographer, to pose at the Clifton overhang, at Mile 8.5. Behind the locomotive and tender are a box car, a baggage car, and two coaches   the rearmost is No. 214, **Lake Spirit**, still in service today.*
Vancouver Public Library
Photograph Number 9762

Opposite: Ninety years later, WP&YR trains still pass under the rock face at Clifton.

Locomotive Works), in early 1982, but just on completion of the locomotives the railway was forced to cancel the order.

These locomotives, which were numbered 111 to 114, were similar to the 101-class diesels; all lay in storage in the Montreal area before finally being sold—three to the U.S Gypsum Corporation in 1991 and 1993, the last one, No. 114, to the WP&YR in 1995.

In 1982 there was still a demand for passenger service, but income from this alone could not possibly sustain the whole operation. In 1981, the last full year of mixed train operation, the WP&YR carried 55,000 passengers—down from the highs of the late 1970s. From October of 1982 until spring of 1988, all WP&YR heavy railway equipment lay idle, its future uncertain.

1988 to date

TOURISM - REBIRTH

In 1985 Curragh Resources acquired the inactive Cyprus Anvil mine, although production did not resume until 1988. But, back in December of 1984 the Canadian Government had already decided to make the South Klondike Highway between Carcross and Skagway a year-round haulage road; it had been completed in 1978 for summer-use only. Cyprus Anvil had always complained that it was "subsidizing" the railway, since the Whitehorse-Skagway section of the haul was by far the most expensive portion of the whole haulage route—Faro to Skagway. When the mine at Faro did reopen, Curragh Resources hired a trucking contractor which hauled concentrates from the Faro mill directly to Skagway, leaving the WP&YR with little or no hope for future freighting. In maintaining the highway, the Canadian Government (in reality Canadian taxpayers) was now subsidizing the mining company. A costly deal.

There was, however, a revival of the coastal tourism business, and cruise ship traffic into Skagway began growing. In spring of 1988, the WP&YR re-opened the twenty-mile stretch of line between Skagway and White Pass for summer-only, passenger-only, business. Eight of the eleven General Electric diesel locomotives, still in the 1980s paint scheme, were once more readied for service. In addition, steam locomotive No. 73 was fired up to transfer trains from the docks to the shops where diesels took over for the run to White Pass. The first train in revenue service since 1982 ran on May 12, 1988.

Two of the General Electric diesels had spent the last six years in storage in Whitehorse, but both were brought over the rough track to Skagway in the fall of 1988. The eight 1200-horsepower locomotives remained idle, at Shops. Then in 1992 numbers 101, 103, 105, 106, and 107 were sold to an operator in Colombia. By 1993 number 108 went to work, joined by 109 and 110 in 1994. When business resumed in 1988, the WP&YR had thirty-four coaches in use. Another eleven were built in 1992 and 1993.

In the first tentative tourism season, late May to end September of 1988, the "new" WP&YR carried more than 39,000 passengers. In the 1989 season, rail service was extended to Fraser, B.C., where connections were made with tour buses, and a service was offered to Bennett to oblige Chilkoot Pass trekkers; that season brought 77,000 patrons. Traffic continued to grow, and during the 1997 season 213,000 satisfied visitors had partaken of the pleasure. Early in 1998 the WP&YR celebrated its 100th birthday.

Narrow gauge railways have always been popular with rail fans and vacationers alike, partly because of their rarity and charm, but also because of the wild and wonderful terrain most of these railways traverse—the WP&YR is loved and extolled around the world. With north-west coast tourism ever-popular, there is good reason to believe the WP&YR will live for yet another 100 years.

People of Today's
White Pass & Yukon Route

Almost from its beginnings Skagway has been a railway town, dependant on the operation of the WP&YR. The railway attracted a special breed of hardy people willing to work, make homes, and raise families, in this remote locale. Today, many Skagwayans are second, third, and even fourth generation "White Passers". Although Whitehorse and other Yukon stations had a significant number of operational and maintenance men, Skagway had by far the largest railway work force. All but a few maintenance-of-way men call Skagway home today.

At Shops, rebuilding and maintenance work keeps mechanics and other craftsmen busy during the off-season. At headquarters in the Skagway station, management is never short of chores, wrapping up last season's work, and planning service for the coming season. For both groups, the touring season is extremely busy and very smoothly organized.

At the throttle of No. 109, engineer Dan Law gives a friendly wave to trackside photographers.

*Steve Burnham touches up the finish on coach No. 214, **Lake Spirit**, being refurbished at the WP&YR shops. The coach is also seen in the photo on page 74.*

The coach is also seen in the photo on page 74.

*Carl Hoover is working on a rebuild of coach No. 264, the **Lake Aishihik**; built in 1884 it is the second oldest coach in the fleet.*

Gerald Revis assembles a new passenger coach truck. Most of the older coaches had aging wood-and-steel trucks, with brass bearings, which are being replaced with all-steel, roller bearing-fitted trucks.

Mechanic Lloyd Sullivan repairs a traction motor from a locomotive truck.

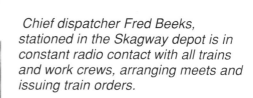

Chief dispatcher Fred Beeks, stationed in the Skagway depot is in constant radio contact with all trains and work crews, arranging meets and issuing train orders.

Carey Born is at work on the fuel injectors of an Alco-engined 90-class diesel-electric locomotive.

Skagway passenger agent Angela Fulmer (left) praises the virtues of the Summit Excursion to Tina Cyr, visitor from afar (in reality Tina is Director of Marketing for the WP&YR at Skagway).

At Bennett, brakeman Jim Roberts has just uncoupled the locomotives from the train. The locomotives will run around the coaches on the siding and recouple on the far end of the train, for the run back to Skagway.

It also takes good track maintenance to keep the trains running. Near Meadows, the Carcross-based track maintenance gang is replacing ties. The crew consists of, from left to right, foreman Charles Johns, John Wally, Patrick James, Richard Atlin, Jack Bogaard, and Ted Huebschwerlen.

WP&YR engineer John Westfall (a young veteran with the railway) at the controls of engine No. 90, northbound to Bennett, enjoys his work.

Equipment of Today's
White Pass & Yukon Route

> Running in such a remote area, the railway of the WP&YR is reminiscent of a slower, simpler, life of days gone by; it is one of the very few operating narrow gauge railways in North America dating from the turn of the century, and utilizes a rustic blend of vintage and new equipment.
>
> Small by modern railway standards, the equipment was designed to traverse steep grades and tight curves, as are found on the WP&YR's scenic, unique, route. Some of the rolling stock was built by WP&YR shop men, and others came from as far away as Newfoundland and Pennsylvania. Many of the passenger coaches are genuine antiques, dating from more than 100 years ago.

Locomotives

Steam locomotive No. 73 was built by the Baldwin Locomotive Works in May, 1947, the last steam locomotive to be acquired by the WP&YR. No. 73 was retired in 1964, and placed on display at Bennett in 1968. In 1982 it was brought back to Skagway where it was rebuilt. In tourist service that year, it operated only a few months, and like the rest of WP&YR's railway equipment, No. 73 went into storage until the reopening of service in 1988.

Diesel-electric locomotives Nos. 91 to 100 weigh in at between 84 and 86 tons, and are rated at 800 to 990 horsepower. All were built by General Electric, although their 6-cylinder diesel engines were built by Alco Products Limited. Construction dates are:

90, 91	June 1954
92, 93, 94	December 1956
95, 96, 97	March 1963
98, 99, 100	May 1966

All except No. 96 are active as of 1998.

Diesel-electric locomotives Nos. 108, 109, and 110 weigh in at 136 tons and are rated at 1200 horsepower. All were built in December, 1971, by the Montreal Locomotive Works and are powered by the company's own Alco 6-cylinder diesels. After the shutdown of 1982, the three locomotives did not return to service until 1993 and 1994. In 1969, seven identical locomotives, Nos. 101 to 107, were built for the WP&YR. Two of them, No. 102 and No. 105, were destroyed in the round house fire of late 1969, and the remaining five were sold to a South American railway in 1992.

All of the 90-class and 101-class locomotives were delivered in the yellow and green colour scheme seen today. Between 1976 and 1979 seven were repainted in a very attractive orange/white/blue scheme. Between 1980 and 1981, all of the active locomotives (No. 96 was unserviceable) were repainted in a rather drab blue and white colour scheme. When WP&YR operations resumed in 1988, only the 90-class locomotives went into service still wearing the 1980 livery. In 1991, WP&YR shops began repainting all of the locomotives (except No. 96) in the original yellow and green scheme, and by 1995 the job was complete.

Diesel-electric locomotive No. 114 and three sister locomotives numbered 111 to 113 were built by Bombardier Inc. (successor to Montreal Locomotive Works) in 1982 for the WP&YR. The order was cancelled when the WP&YR was forced to suspend operations, and the locomotives remained in the Montreal area for ten years. The first three were purchased in 1991 and 1992 by the U.S. Gypsum Corporation in California, and No. 114 was finally bought by the WP&YR in 1995. All were delivered in the blue and white scheme of 1980. Except for the cabs and trucks, the locomotives are nearly identical to Nos. 108 to 110.

Steam pressure in No. 73's oil-fired boiler has built up and is being automatically relieved in a hissing blast.

At Shops, the WP&YR's maintenance centre, a complete rebuilding and servicing facility, locomotives and cars are kept in top condition. Too distant from American and Canadian railway maintenance and building centres, the WP&YR shops developed into a versatile and self-sufficient operation.

Although built for the WP&YR in 1982, locomotive No. 114 did not reach Skagway until 1995, and it was not put into service until 1996.

In summer of 1992, this string of locomotives has been out of service since the shutdown of 1982. Parked at Shops midst grass and dandelions going to seed are Nos. 101, 103, 104, 106, 109, 110, 107, and 108; within a few months five of them would be gone, sold to a railway in Colombia. The remaining three, Nos. 108, 109, and 110, would not be put to full service on the White Pass until 1994.

The first locomotive to arrive at Skagway survives today. Built in 1881 by Brooks, the locomotive first saw service on the Utah and Northern Railway. After completion of the railway of the WP&YR in 1900, the locomotive was little used, but in 1931 it was barged to Taku where for another six summer seasons it worked the WP&YR's Taku Tram, serving the Atlin goldfield. For more than twenty-eight years, No. 52 lay derelict at isolated Taku. Then, in March of 1963, the old Brooks was recovered by a Skagway group led by Carl Mulvihill and brought to Skagway where it was cosmetically restored, eventually to be placed on display across the street from the WP&YR station—where it is seen today.

Passenger Coaches

Passenger cars are a mixture of new and some very old cars, constructed by various car builders—such as Carter, Hammond, and Pullman—of the early days of railroading in the United States. Some of the older cars were built by the WP&YR at Skagway while others first went into service on "lower 48" railways such as, the Sumpter Valley in Oregon, the Pacific Coast Railway in California, and the Columbia and Puget Sound in Washington. All of the older cars have been rebuilt over the years. Only one cupola-equipped baggage/coach (combo) remains on the fleet. Among the newest cars are some which are wheelchair-accessible.

No.	Name	Year Built	No.	Name	Year Built
200	Lake Summit	1992	244	Lake Emerald	1883
201	Lake Crater	1992	248	Lake Tagish	1887
202	Lake Bare Loon	1992	252	Lake Muncho	1893
203	Lake Fantail	1993	254	Lake Dezadeash	1893
204	Lake Chilkoot	1993	256	Lake Laberge	1936
205	Lake Chilkat	1993	258	Lake Kluahne	1893
206	Lake Nares	1993	260	Lake Tutshi	1893
207	Lake Morrow	1993	264	Lake Aishihik	1884
208	Lake Homan	1993	266	Lake Schwatka	1917
209	Lake Bernard	1993	267	Lake Portage	1918
211	no name, baggage-coach	1918	268	Lake Lewes	1917
214	Lake Spirit	pre-1900	270	Lake Kathleen	1893
216	Lake Black	pre-1900	272	Lake Nisutlin	1900
218	Lake Atlin	1889	274	Lake Primrose	1969
220	Lake Dewey	1889	276	Lake Big Salmon	1969
222	Lake Lindeman	1889	278	Lake Fairweather	1969
224	Lake Marsh	1889	280	Lake Dease	1969
226	Lake Fraser	1903	282	Lake Klukshu	1976
234	Lake Cowley	pre-1916	284	Lake Takhini	1976
236	Lake Mayo	pre-1916	286	Lake Kusawa	1976
238	Lake Watson	1922	288	Lake McClintock	1976
240	Lake Bennett	pre-1926	290	Yukon River	1993
242	Lake Teslin	pre-1926			

Lake Fraser, coach No. 226, was built by WP&YR shop men in 1903. Note the down-curved roof and clerestory at the ends of the coach.

Lake Tagish, coach No. 248, is the third oldest coach of the WP&YR's fleet, having been built in 1887 for the South Pacific Coast Railroad. It was acquired by the WP&YR in 1928 specially for the WP&YR-operated Taku Tram where it served until late 1936. Compare the straight roof line with that of No. 226. No. 248, like most of the WP&YR's other older cars, was originally a parlour car, in that there were no fixed bench seats, but casually-placed wicker chairs.

Maintenance-of-Way Equipment

Seen prominently in front of the Skagway depot is a Cooke rotary snowplow, WP&YR No. 1, built in 1898. In use every season until 1962 when bulldozers took over its duties, No. 1 was then retired and left at Bennett. Later returned to Shops, it was rebuilt over the winter of 1995-96 and went to work that spring, clearing snow on either side of White Pass. Since then, No. 1 has been in service every April, and for the remaining months is parked on display in Skagway for the benefit of visitors.

The WP&YR has a number of pieces of rail service equipment for maintenance of the line. Included in this list are depressed centre flat cars for hauling bulldozers and other heavy machinery up-line. Prominent because of their bright orange paint jobs are gondolas for hauling ballast. These cars were acquired from the 42-inch gauge Newfoundland Railway and retrucked to 36-inch gauge. Then there is the fleet of orange rail motor cars, also known as Casey cars or speeders, used by foremen and maintenance-of-way gangs. Like major railways elsewhere, the WP&YR is fully-equipped for any and all line construction and repair.

WP&YR section gangs get to the job site with these gas-powered speeders

The WP&YR has obtained equipment from far and wide. These gondolas came from the Newfoundland Railway.

89

Old wooden caboose No. 909 was brought to Skagway in the war years by the US Army, having served on the Sumpter Valley Railway in Oregon. The ghost image of the Thunderbird, a symbol of the WP&YR since the 1950s, was visible on the caboose in 1991.

Another narrow gauge railway once operated in the Yukon Territory. Built in 1906, the Klondike Mines Railway operated out of Dawson City, into the Klondike goldfield, for only eight seasons before being shut down. The railway was equipped with rebuilt and remanufactured equipment provided by the WP&YR; among the locomotives were ex-WP&YR No. 63, No. 55, and No. 57 (the latter is seen on page 67 of **The Sea-to-Sky Gold Rush Route**). A fourth locomotive, KMR No. 4, was bought new in 1912, and was purchased by the WP&YR in 1942 for use during the hectic Alcan Highway construction period. Remarkably, all four locomotives survive today. The railway also had twenty-three freight cars, which were built by the WP&YR in Skagway. For the full story of this little-known gold rush railway, see:

The Bonanza Narrow Gauge Railway
The Story of the Klondike Mines Railway

by Eric L. Johnson. Copies of this fully-illustrated, 176-page, softcover book are available for $19.95 (US funds) plus $3.50 for shipping from the publisher:

Rusty Spike Publishing
112 - 2320 West 40th Avenue,
Vancouver, B.C.,
Canada   V6M 4H6

Rusty Spike Publishing